"Multiplying movements are the ke[...] *Pioneering Movements*, Steve Addison unpacks the leadership required to spark and sustain movements of disciples and churches. I love this book! It is biblically sound, practical and inspiring."

David Garrison, author of *A Wind in the House of Islam*

"With sensitivity to history and an ability to extract principles from the lives of the apostolic pioneers who have gone before us, Steve gives us an inspirational peek into movements and the people who lead them."

Alan Hirsch, founder of Forge Mission Training Network, author of *The Forgotten Ways* and *The Permanent Revolution*

"*Pioneering Movements* paints a picture of the difference between spiritual leaders who start churches and those who launch movements. Addison provides a delicious cross-section of the traits, efforts and focus of men and women, expatriates and nationals who cross that line to spark movements that change their worlds."

Steve Smith, global CPM catalyst, author of *T4T*

"The best thing about this book is the stories and the people—it's all real! This isn't wishful idealism or bland theology. With the type of leadership Steve describes and the powerful presence of the Spirit of God, movements are possible, and God expects and even longs for our participation. As a practitioner, Steve gives us plenty of 'how-tos.' The choice to engage is ours."

Sam Metcalf, president, CRM-US, author of *Beyond the Local Church*

"Steve Addison's third book on movements builds on his previous writings by inviting Christ followers to become 'movement pioneers' wherever they live. *Pioneering Movements* is filled with examples of such people from the early church, Christian history and modern-day movements. Steve makes a compelling case that God can use any Christ follower for disciple making, while also providing simple, practical steps to get started."

Jerry Trousdale, author of *Miraculous Movements*

"The history of global missions is rich and encouraging. Even in this complex age we can learn a great deal from those who have gone before. In *Pioneering Movements*, Steve Addison provides us with a compelling reminder of the important role godly leaders play in the proliferation of the gospel for God's glory. Addison's book is both instructive and inspirational."

Ed Stetzer, executive director, LifeWay Research

"Hundreds of thousands of books will be published this year, but only a few have the potential to change the world. This latest book by Steve Addison is one of those few books. Movements of all kinds change our world on a daily basis. Pioneering movements of discipleship are the most powerful movements of all because they change communities of people at the heart level. What Steve has created is a manual to help all of us become the pioneers of these world-changing movements. This book is an essential resource for the missions community."

Rick Wood, editor, *Mission Frontiers* magazine

PIONEERING MOVEMENTS

Leadership That Multiplies Disciples and Churches

. . . .

STEVE ADDISON

Foreword by DAVE FERGUSON

IVP Books

An imprint of InterVarsity Press
Downers Grove, Illinois

InterVarsity Press
P.O. Box 1400, Downers Grove, IL 60515-1426
ivpress.com
email@ivpress.com

InterVarsity Press® is the book-publishing division of InterVarsity Christian Fellowship/USA®, a movement of students and faculty active on campus at hundreds of universities, colleges and schools of nursing in the United States of America, and a member movement of the International Fellowship of Evangelical Students. For information about local and regional activities, visit intervarsity.org.

All Scripture quotations, unless otherwise indicated, are taken from THE HOLY BIBLE, NEW INTERNATIONAL VERSION®, NIV® Copyright © 1973, 1978, 1984, 2011 by Biblica, Inc.™ Used by permission. All rights reserved worldwide.

While any stories in this book are true, some names and identifying information may have been changed to protect the privacy of individuals.

Figure 2.1 on p. 40 is adapted and used by permission from Steve Addison, What Jesus Started (Downers Grove, IL: InterVarsity Press, 2012), p. 17.

Figure 3.1 on p. 56 is adapted and used by permission from Paul Barnett, Jesus and the Rise of Early Christianity (Downers Grove, IL: IVP Academic, 1999), p. 236.

Figure 6.7 on p. 104 is adapted and used by permission from Nathan Shank and Kari Shank, "Four Fields of Kingdom Growth: Starting and Releasing Healthy Churches," Movements.net, www.movements.net/4fields2014.

Figure 9.1 on p. 147 is reproduced by permission from David Garrison, A Wind in the House of Islam (Monument, CO: WIGTake Resources, 2014).

Cover design: Cindy Kiple
Interior design: Beth McGill
Images: © li jingwang/iStockphoto
Maps and diagrams: Peter Bergmeier

ISBN 978-0-8308-4441-8 (print)
ISBN 978-0-8308-9897-8 (digital)

Printed in the United States of America ∞

Library of Congress Cataloging-in-Publication Data

Addison, Steve.
  Pioneering movements : leadership that multiplies disciples and churches / Steve Addison.
     pages cm
  Includes bibliographical references.
  ISBN 978-0-8308-4441-8 (pbk. : alk. paper)
  1. Discipling (Christianity) 2. Evangelistic work. 3. Missions. 4. Church history. I. Title.
  BV4520.A25 2015
  269'.2--dc23
                                                                                              2015033683

P   21   20   19   18   17   16   15   14   13   12   11   10   9   8   7   6   5   4   3   2   1
Y   33   32   31   30   29   28   27   26   25   24   23   22   21   20   19   18   17   16   15

To Bill Smith

To Bill Smith

Contents

Contents

Fixing our eyes on Jesus,
the pioneer and perfecter of faith.

Hebrews 12:2

Foreword

Dave Ferguson

When I first stumbled upon Steve Addison's blog at movements
.net it was like finding a long-lost brother—albeit a more
traveled, more experienced and much smarter brother. From
then on I started routinely checking Steve's latest posts. My
kinship with him grew through our mutual passion and interest in movements. Through his writings, and without Steve
knowing it, we became blood brothers with hearts beating fast
to see the church realize its forgotten way as a transformative
movement.

So, when I was given the opportunity to write and publish on
the topic of movements and I needed some brotherly advice, I
called Steve Addison. When I needed someone to challenge the
church planters and network leaders within NewThing (the
movement I lead) I asked Steve to teach us. As I made plans for
the next Exponential conference, where our mission is to ac-
celerate movements, I read everything that Steve put out for
wisdom and guidance. While we live half a world apart, Steve
and I share the same spiritual family and I proudly call him a
brother in this great cause of Christ.

Like an older brother, he is once again a step ahead schooling us on the topic of movements. As you read *Pioneering Movements* you will discover three truths about movement making:

1. Movements are led by apostolic leaders. In *Pioneering Movements*, Addison does a great job of pointing to Jesus as our pioneering apostle and then helps us immensely by giving us both biblical and historical examples of apostolic leadership. In so doing, Steve presents a strong case that the church will not experience accelerated Great Commission expansion in the absence of this type of leadership. In fact, the greater the missional impact, the more obvious the pioneering apostolic leadership becomes. As a person who feels called to identify, equip and commission apostolic leaders, this will be a book that I will read and re-read. I will also pass along this book to church planters and network leaders within my influence because those with a pioneering gift need to understand the importance of their calling to the mission.

2. Movement is God's means for accomplishing the mission of Jesus. Jesus challenges us in Acts 1:8 with a vision of a church on the move. As Jesus paints a picture of a preferable future, we see the church moving from Jerusalem, throughout Judea, Samaria and the uttermost parts of the world. Jesus left us with a vision for how his movement could accomplish the mission. Addison takes that vision and brilliantly gives us both strategy and story to show us the way. I absolutely love chapter six, where he explains the five levels of movement leadership. I can't wait to pass along that piece of developmental strategy to the men and women I am training to start networks and movements. Wisely, Steve goes beyond just strategy and supports it with real-world stories of pioneering leaders God has used around the world. As

you read *Pioneering Movements*, you will be convicted that movement is not just the latest buzzword or trendy phrase; it is how God wants to accomplish his mission.

3. Movements are not just a topic to research, but a way to join God in his great redemptive work. My favorite line in this book is, "I was an expert, but I wasn't living it out." What you are reading is a rarity because the author refuses to let movement become merely an academic project. It is rare because this book was written by a gentleman who knows as much about the Christian movement as anyone in the world, and at the same time is daring to put each teaching into practice. It is my hope and prayer that you will do the same. Do not just read these words. Follow Steve's example and attempt to live them out. The insights in this book are from a brother of ours who understands how our ever-expanding and always-including family of God was meant to live and thrive.

For all those reasons and more, it is a great honor for me to recommend to you this great contribution to the mission of Jesus, my brother Steve Addison's *Pioneering Movements: Leadership That Multiplies Disciples and Churches.*

Introduction

> *The spontaneous expansion of the Church reduced to its*
> *element is a very simple thing. It asks for no elaborate*
> *organization, no large finances, no great numbers of*
> *paid missionaries. . . . What is necessary is faith.*

Roland Allen, *The Spontaneous*
Expansion of the Church

For better or for worse, movements create and remake the world we live in. If we want to change the world, we must understand movements. In simple terms, a movement is a group of people committed to changing the world. The spheres of politics, science, culture and faith are shaped and remade by movements.

Jesus founded the greatest movement this world has ever seen. That movement has at its heart the multiplication of disciples and churches—everywhere. As the risen Lord, he still leads the way. This is a book for people who want to obey his command "Come, follow me," and claim his promise "and I will teach you to fish for people."

Ten years ago I had just come out of China and was passing through Singapore. There I met with two men, both named Smith. They trained and coached leaders across Asia who were multiplying disciples and churches. I was a student of movements; they knew movements from the inside. I shared with them what I had learned about the *five characteristics of dynamic movements*—white-hot faith, commitment to a cause, contagious relationships, rapid mobilization and adaptive methods. Bill Smith and Steve Smith said I had done a good job. Their experience validated my research.

My trip to China had left me wondering whether my *five* characteristics should really be *six*. I felt I should add a crucial sixth characteristic—pioneering or apostolic leadership. When I asked for their opinion, they said, "We have never seen a church-planting movement without apostolic leadership."

That's why I wrote this book.

This is my third book on movements. The first, *Movements That Change the World*, introduced the concept of movements and identified five characteristics of dynamic movements. The second, *What Jesus Started*, followed Jesus' ministry as the founder of a disciple-making movement in the Gospels. That book also addressed how the risen Lord continued his ministry through the Spirit and the Word in the church in Acts. The book revealed how Jesus has been at work multiplying disciples and churches throughout history and around the world today.

Pioneering Movements is a book about leadership, specifically movement leadership. Not movements in a general sense but movements that make disciples and multiply communities of Jesus' followers. Everywhere. That's what Jesus did. It's what he trained his disciples to do. It's what he is doing today.

WHAT TO EXPECT

In *What Jesus Started* I examined Jesus as the founder of a missionary movement who equipped the Twelve, the early church and Paul as movement pioneers. This book will build on that foundation.

I'm going to begin by sharing some of my journey. Before Jesus was a movement leader he was an obedient Son. We all have to learn that mission is not just an academic pursuit or a theoretical discussion of ministry models, it's about who we are and what we do. We'll never understand pioneering movements unless God shapes us from the inside out.

We'll explore the example of Simon Peter, a neglected figure in Protestantism due to the prominence of Paul. Peter was a natural leader among Jesus' disciples and the founding leader of the Christian movement following Pentecost. He was chosen by God as the bridge between the Jewish and Gentile missions of the early church.

Along the way, we will examine a few of the many case studies of movement pioneers in history and around the world today. In two extended case studies (South Asia and the United States) we'll see what it takes for a movement to get to multiple generations of disciples and churches. I've intentionally chosen one case study from the developing world and one from the Western world. Both movements have broken through to multiple generations of new disciples and new churches.

For security reasons there is not a lot of detailed information available on pioneering movements among Muslims. So I've spoken privately with those who have firsthand experience and discovered that there is an unprecedented number of disciple-making movements among Muslims around the world.

We'll examine the relationship between movement pioneers, their teams and the local churches. We'll ask, How can we align our current church and mission structures to take advantage of this important leadership gift?

We'll look at the five levels of pioneering leadership in a multiplying movement and discover how we can grow leaders at every level. We'll review cases studies of churches who are catalysts for disciple-making movements. We'll explore the authority of apostolic ministry in weakness and in power.

Jesus founded a missionary movement that has spread throughout the world. It is God's mission; it will not cease until that day when every knee will bow and every tongue confess that Jesus Christ is Lord, to the glory of God the Father. The living Lord calls us to partner with him in redeeming a lost world.

one

Movement Pioneers Lead from the Inside Out

Some practitioners spend too much effort trying to get the strategy and methodology right rather than looking for the right person to invest in. If someone says to me, give me the method or give me the curriculum, I know they have not understood that this is accomplished through persons rather than through methods.

Bill Smith

I've devoted most of my adult life to wrestling with how God works through movements. My interest isn't purely academic. I believe Jesus Christ is the only hope for a lost world.

I knew more about movements than anyone else I knew. But knowledge was not enough. This is the first lesson of pioneering movements. It has nothing to do with what we bring to the table. It has everything to do with God. So despite my knowledge and experience, my life and ministry had to be remade from the inside out. That's not easy.

Change is hard, not just because we have to embrace a new thing. Change is hard because we have to let go of the old thing.

To remake our ministry, we have to die before we can live again. This is the story of how God remade me from the inside out. These are the lessons I learned about the journey from armchair expert to movement pioneer.

LET GOD HAVE HIS WAY

In August 2008, I hit a wall. Actually, I'd been hitting it for some time. This time I didn't get up.

I have a history of depression, but I can manage it and keep functioning until the cloud lifts. Not this time. I found myself in a very dark and frightening place, not knowing if I would ever climb out of it. If 10 is the best a person could ever be, and 1 is the worst, I was a 2. All I could do was get through one day at a time—sometimes an hour at a time. For months I didn't believe there was any way back.

My wife, Michelle, was amazing. She never lost faith in me and supported me through the whole time. Leaders and friends at our local church went out of their way to encourage and support me. Friends and colleagues from around Australia and beyond left me in no doubt that I would rebound.

I was the leader, and still am, of MOVE, an Australian-based mission agency. I told my board that I wasn't sure I could continue in my role. The board stood by me and allowed me the time I needed to recover. I sought professional help from a Christian psychiatrist and a Christian counselor.

The book of Job became a constant companion. It's as though I discovered it for the first time. With Job I poured out my heart to God in bewilderment and confusion. As with Job, there were no answers, or at least not the ones I wanted. God did not rescue me, at least not in the way I wanted. I felt like God had abandoned me, and yet somehow I clung to God and trusted that he is faithful and just.

I remember sitting in my psychiatrist's office fishing for some sympathy. I told him I thought my life was over. I would grow old without ever seeing my dreams fulfilled. My life would have no legacy. He looked straight at me and said, "Who promised you a legacy? Who promised you purpose?" He opened his desk drawer and drew out a pocket New Testament and began reading me verses on the love of God. There was no guarantee of the legacy I wanted. There was no guarantee of the purpose I felt was my due, just the promise of the everlasting love of God in Christ.

That was the turning point. I told God, "If that's the deal, then I'm up for it. Even if every day is filled with feelings of despair, I will trust you. Even if I never see my dreams fulfilled, I will serve you." I doubted everything except the reality of Jesus' death and resurrection, and the promise of God's love. That was enough.

In October, November and December 2008, I hung on as best I could as things slowly began to improve. By February 2009 I was back in the game of life. It had taken me six months to recover.

I didn't just recover. I had been profoundly changed. There was a deep conviction about the reality of God's love and his ultimate victory over evil. I knew that God had his hand on my life and had set me aside for a purpose—but on his terms. My life was firmly in his hands.

I felt I had lost everything and found God. Now everything I had was a gift, not a possession. Life had thrown its worst at me, and I had survived. The depression could come back, but I wasn't afraid of it anymore. I felt free and dangerous. Somehow, this experience prepared me for some profound

shifts in how God worked through me in multiplying disciples and churches.

God can use times of crisis to remake leaders from the inside
out. At first everything is fine. Church leaders have effective
ministries and no big questions that need answers. They have a
way of seeing the world, and it makes sense. Then God unsettles
them. Sometimes, it's a personal crisis. Sometimes, it's a ministry
crisis. It may be a growing sense that there has to be more. For
whatever reason, they are unfrozen. Like the children of Israel
in the wilderness, the leader can't go back, and they don't know
how to go forward. They're lost.

We may think of the wilderness as a place to avoid, a place
of testing. Yet the wilderness is also a place where we encounter God. It is a place of profound change. We are given
the opportunity to surrender and trust God before there are
any answers. Pass that test and clarity will come as a byproduct
of surrender.

Most movement pioneers have faced God in the wilderness
and allowed him to remake them. Breakthroughs in pioneering
movements often occur as the byproduct of crisis encounters
with God.

BEGIN BY DOING SOMETHING

A year after my recovery, my first book, *Movements That Change
the World*, was published. To my surprise and delight, people
bought it. I was riding high on the success of that book when
the next breakthrough came. God spoke to me through my wife,
Michelle. I wasn't ready for what she had to say: "You've written
a great book, Steve! But when are you going to do something?"
I wanted to be offended, but I knew God was speaking to me

through Michelle. I knew all the movement principles, but I didn't really know them. I was the expert, but I wasn't living them out. God was rattling my cage. *Knowing* something was not enough; he wanted me to *do* something.

I could have been in the running as the world's worst evangelist. It had been years since I led someone to Christ. It wasn't my gift. And I was already too busy leading a mission agency to share the gospel with people!

We lived just a few minutes' drive from Box Hill in Melbourne. Box Hill is home to thousands of immigrants and international students from across the globe. The largest group is from mainland China. God had brought the world to our doorstep.

So Michelle and I set off one Sunday afternoon to walk around the shopping district of Box Hill, praying, sharing and looking for people of peace who wanted to learn more about Jesus. On the very first afternoon God led us to someone who wanted to know more and who introduced us to her relational world. For eight years we had lived just a few minutes from Box Hill, and the first time we attempted to connect with people and share the gospel, God showed up.

It changes you when you share the gospel with a young Chinese couple who has just arrived in Melbourne to begin their new lives. It changes you when they finally accept Christ and you baptize them in the local swimming pool. You're never the same when they begin sharing with their friends and your small discipleship group forms into a new church.

I'm still not the world's best evangelist. In fact, if there's a gift, I don't have it. I'm the guy who prays for an empty seat next to me on the airplane so I can read. But I've learned to connect with people, share the gospel, train disciples and form new churches. I'm still wrestling with how we get to multiplication, but that's okay. I've made a start.

Before, I had understood movements from the outside. Now, I have begun to understand movements from the inside. It began with a step of obedience.

I talk to a lot of leaders who are stuck. They think they have to rewire their whole lives and ministries before they can implement change. It's the all-or-nothing syndrome. If we can't do it all, we'll do nothing. In response I tell them, "Don't change anything about your life or ministry. Don't impose this on your unsuspecting congregation. Just free up two hours a week, find a partner and begin doing it yourself. See what God does, then build on that. Take a step of obedience, watch what God does and build on that. Now, you're ready for some training."

TRAIN, TRAIN, TRAIN

I've been a youth worker, a church planter, a pastor and a missionary. I've discovered many of us don't know what to do on Monday morning. We know Jesus' prime directive is to go and make disciples. That's what we signed up to do. But no one has shown us how—what to do on Monday morning. So, we fall back into running programs, or we focus on secondary goals. So little of our time makes a difference when it comes to obeying the Great Commission.

We may know how to motivate and exhort, but not how to train and to do. So the people we lead are passive or guilt-ridden. I tell pastors, "If you exhort your people without training them, you're setting them up for failure and guilt. You're also creating a dependency relationship in which you, as the professional, do the ministry on their behalf."

Training followed by action breaks this cycle. Teach people to share their stories and the gospel story and they have something they can do. When they step out in obedience, they see God at work and their faith grows. There's no turning back when they've led someone to Christ. They'll never be the same after they baptize that person and begin teaching him or her how to follow Jesus. They won't need external motivators anymore.

Real learning takes place in the field, but training gives confidence to step out and do something so on-the-job learning can begin. I brought Jeff Sundell to Australia to train and to run summits for practitioners. He had spent ten years as a movement pioneer among Tibetan Buddhists in northern India and Nepal.[1] In 2009 Jeff and Angie Sundell moved back to the United States and began applying movement principles in a Western setting.

As Jeff passed on what he was learning, we discovered that the same principles could apply in Australia. The circle of practitioners kept widening. There's now a national network of people who are putting the training into practice. They are seeing people come to faith and move into discipleship groups, and new churches have been formed.

We also decided to bring out Bill Smith, who led us in twelve days of training. When I look back, the content was important, but what really made a difference was Bill—his heart for God and his love for lost people. Because he has devoted his life to empowering leaders for church-planting movements—he has been training and coaching movement pioneers longer than anyone I know—he speaks with authority.

I got the right people in the room. I was the catalyst and they would be the practitioners, or so I thought. On the last day of the training with Bill, we laid out our plans for Australia. I knew my role: I would cast vision. I would get others on board. I would network them. I would bring out practitioners to train and develop our own trainers. But God had other plans. As we committed our plans to prayer, God spoke to my heart and said, "I want you to train, train, train across Australia for the next eighteen months and then stop."

And that's what I did. It was June 2012. I had until the end of 2013, so I cleared my calendar and started calling around, seeking opportunities to train others in multiplying disciples and churches. I looked at the best practice examples of training for multiplication and developed my own version called "Following and Fishing." The title was based on Jesus' command, "Come, follow me," and his promise, "I will send you out to fish for people" (Mark 1:17).

The training approach assumes that we've spent too much time trying to motivate people to make disciples and not enough time training them. People know what they should do, but don't know how to do it. The learning is hands-on and immediately applicable. We teach how to connect with people, pray for a need and then ask, "Are you near or far from God? Would you like to be nearer?"

We teach them how to share their story of faith in Christ in three minutes and how to share a gospel story of someone who was far from God and came near to him. They learn how to share a gospel outline and lead someone to Christ. They also learn how to help someone become a follower of Jesus through Discovery Bible Study, a method of making disciples that was pioneered by David Watson and has spread all over the world.[2]

Discovery Bible Study is a simple yet powerful method of helping people encounter Jesus in the Scriptures and learn to follow and obey him. We read a passage and ask, What do we learn about God? What do we learn about the people in the passage? We discuss how we will obey what the passage says. We commit to share with someone what we've learned, and we pray for each other. Scripture is the teacher. Everyone is a participant. The focus is on obedience to God's Word. The goal of connecting and sharing is to form obedience-oriented discipleship groups that can become church.[3] (See the appendix for more information on how to conduct this method of study.)

I determined to accept every opportunity to train I could, if it was humanly possible. Things started slowly, and then my calendar began to fill. In Melbourne I trained during eight weekly sessions and on two to three separate weekends, I also crisscrossed Australia, training interstate.

We covered how to share one's story and God's story (the gospel), how to pray for lost people by name, how to facilitate a Discovery Bible Study for people far from God and for new disciples, how to form discipleship groups that become churches, and how to multiply workers. All the training was hands-on and to be applied between sessions.

I trained in Melbourne, Sydney, Wollongong, Perth, Adelaide, Brisbane, Hobart, Launceston, Ballarat, Toowoomba, Surfers Paradise and Canberra. I've trained groups of as few as two and sizable groups in some of the largest churches in Australia. I've trained Baptists, Churches of Christ, Pentecostals, Salvation Army, Anglicans, house churches, organic churches, independent churches and those AWOL from church. Hundreds of people were trained.

I learned a few things about training. Most important was to cast a broad net. We need to train a large number of people to find the few who are ready and willing to implement. Just about everyone I trained loved the experience. They all felt more confident in sharing the gospel and making disciples. But only 10–12 percent of the people who attended made a sustained effort to implement the training. There are two ways to look at that ratio. We could despair and say, "Only 10–12 percent!" Or we could say, "As many as 10–12 percent! That means if I train one thousand people, I'll have at least one hundred workers I can teach to train others." I took the second position.

WATCH FOR PEOPLE WHO DO SOMETHING

Joy was one of the people I trained. She is a legal secretary in her thirties living in Melbourne. She was born to farmers in a remote Chinese village, near the border of Russia. Joy accepted Christ in Beijing in 2003 and immediately shared her new faith with her family. Her mother accepted Christ and joined a local house church. Four years later the church was scattered and closed when the government redeveloped the town.

Joy stayed in touch with her mother and tried to encourage her to read the Bible and pray, but she wasn't sure how. She tried to share her faith with the rest of the family, but didn't know what to say. She asked God to send a messenger to help her family follow Jesus. God answered her prayer in a surprising way.

Joy attended the Following and Fishing training at her local church in Melbourne. She learned how to share her story and the gospel story, and how to facilitate Discovery Bible Studies for new disciples. Joy practiced baptizing new believers and helping a discipleship group become a church.

After the first week of training, Joy called her mom and asked if she wanted to read the Bible together over the phone. Her brother and twelve-year-old nephew joined in, and they began studying Mark's Gospel. After reading a passage, Joy would ask the discovery questions: What do you learn about Jesus or God in the story? What do you learn about the people? Is there an example to follow or a command to obey? What will you do to obey what you've learned? With whom will you share this story? How can we pray for each other?

On the second week, Joy's brother confessed his need for forgiveness and surrendered his life to Jesus. Joy thought, *There's no church in my family's town. I can't hang up without my brother being baptized.* So, she asked her mother to get a large bucket of water. While her mother poured the water over her brother, thousands of miles away, Joy pronounced, "In the name of the Father, the Son and the Holy Spirit, I baptize you!"

Joy later told me, "I knew it was not me who baptized my brother. It was the Holy Spirit! It was the Lord who prepared my brother." Then she asked me, "Steve, did I do the right thing?"

I responded, "What does the Bible say?"

"Steve, there are no mobile phones in the Bible!"

So I said, "Joy, was your brother lost and is now found? Was he dead and is now alive?"

"Yes," she said.

"You did the right thing," I assured her.

At first Joy's dad was willing, out of politeness, to participate in the Bible studies over the phone. But he soon pulled back. Then her father saw God's work when Joy's prayers for the provision of an apartment for her parents were answered in an amazing way. As they celebrated the breakthrough, Joy asked her dad if he was ready to accept Christ as his Savior and Lord.

He said yes! Joy asked her mother to get some water, and she baptized her dad over the phone.

There is no church in the village, so Joy is taking her father, her mother, her brother and his wife, and her nephew through basic discipleship. Then she's going to help them plant a church in their village.

The more we trained, the more we found people like Joy who were both faithful and fruitful. Across Australia there is a growing network of people like Joy who are sharing the gospel, making disciples and forming new churches. Movement pioneers are emerging.

MOVE now has workers in Australia, the South Pacific, Thailand, India and the United Kingdom who are fueling church-planting movements through local partners.

LAY DOWN TRACKS FOR THE TRAIN TO RUN ON

I remember our first training group of just eight participants. One was a pastor who took exception to learning how to share his story in three minutes or less. He felt it was formulaic. Two weeks later he was back with news. His ninety-year-old father had never understood his son's faith. Now, for the first time, this pastor had shared his story with his father, who had listened intently.

Methods matter. They have to be simple but profound. Teaching every believer to share his or her story is simple and easy—and profound. Every believer has a story, and stories touch the heart in a way that arguments never can.

We have to find simple but profound methods that are contagious. They can spread to new and existing believers quickly and effectively. Some of these are:

- How to pray for a need and ask, "Are you near or far from God right now?"
- How to share a story from the life of Jesus.
- How to facilitate a Discovery Bible Study in a home.
- How to lead someone to Christ.
- How to use Discovery Bible Study to disciple new believers.
- How to help a discipleship group become a church.

Once we identify people who are sharing the gospel and making disciples, we need simple methods to equip and encourage them. Once or twice a month we get together for an hour and a half, and we help each other reflect and refocus by asking,

- What have you done since we last met?
- How have you seen God at work?
- What are you learning?
- Where are you stuck?
- What do you need to do next?
- How can we pray for you?

Once or twice a year we go away for two to three days and follow the same pattern of reporting what's happening, mutual learning, identifying obstacles and prayerfully moving forward. These simple but profound gatherings of practitioners are the engine room of a movement. Out of such gatherings movement pioneers emerge who have a "no place left" calling for their city, region or nation.

GIVE GOD SOME ROOM TO MOVE

While all this was going on, I spent much time reflecting on Jesus as the founder of a movement in the Gospels and Acts.

Out of that experience, I wrote *What Jesus Started*. I realized that if it all had been up to the disciples, the Christian movement would never have gotten off the ground. The disciples would have finished their lives remembering the good old days when Jesus was alive, wondering what could have been. Instead, Jesus rose from the dead, gathered them together, and over forty days taught them what they needed to know. Then he sent the Holy Spirit. I realized I was no better than those first disciples. It's not up to me. I learned to delight in my weakness and cast myself on God, who raised Jesus from the dead.

The book of Acts is not about how good the apostles were. It's not about the mission of the church. Acts is about the ongoing ministry of Jesus, the risen Lord. Acts tells the story of the growth, the spread and the multiplication of the dynamic Word of God. The Word is an unstoppable force. Wherever the Word goes, people far from God are saved, disciples are made and new churches are formed.

There was opposition. There was suffering. There was sin and failure among God's people. But the Word continued to advance. Mission is not about us; it's about God. He calls us to join as obedient disciples in what he is doing. By his grace it's a partnership in which we make a real contribution, but it's his mission.

That's why we begin by putting aside all excuses about what we can and can't do. We have to put aside our mission and our gospel and do what Paul did on the road to Damascus. He humbled himself before the risen Lord Jesus and heard his call:

> Now get up and stand on your feet. I have appeared to you
> to appoint you as a servant and as a witness of what you

have seen and will see of me. I will rescue you from your own people and from the Gentiles. I am sending you to them to open their eyes and turn them from darkness to light, and from the power of Satan to God, so that they may receive forgiveness of sins and a place among those who are sanctified by faith in me. (Acts 26:16-18)

Paul tells us he wasted no time in obeying Jesus' call. He immediately began proclaiming the gospel. We must begin at the same place and expect God to work wonders as we obey him.

That's my journey from armchair expert to movement pioneer. When it began, I had already written a book on movements. I wasn't lacking information; my head was full of knowledge. God needed to do a deep work in my heart first, and then he trained my hands. Soon I was helping others get started. Something changes in us when we see people who are far from God discover Jesus for themselves. We change as we help them on the journey of learning how to follow and obey him. We change when new disciples discover what it means to belong to the people of God. We change when the workers we train begin making disciples and planting churches. It's hard work, but it's worth it.

WE CAN MOVE ON NOW, OR I COULD SHARE THE GOSPEL

In January 2014 I fulfilled a lifelong dream: I went trekking in the Himalayas. With me were coworkers from Australia, the United States, Bhutan and India.

As we walked, India was on one side of the track; Nepal was on the other. Every day we had to check in at an army post to have our border permits and passports checked. When we arrived at an army post, the soldiers would come out to see what was going on and talk in Hindi to Nathan and our guides.

At one checkpoint, we'd just finished the paperwork when Nathan called us together and said, "We can move on now, or I could share the gospel." We agreed to stop and let him share in Hindi while one of the guides translated for us in English.

He asked each soldier which state of India he called home. He told them we were from different nations. He told them we had come together for a spiritual purpose: to walk, enjoy creation and pray to the Creator. He asked if they knew the Creator God. He then explained that the God who created all things is all-powerful, divine and all-wise. This God does not need service from humanity, but he desires a relationship with us, his creatures. Nothing in creation can contain him, not even an idol.

The soldiers stood silently, listening to the gospel in the biting cold.

Finally, we lined up as a group and shook the hand of every soldier, each one smiling and nodding in appreciation that we had taken the time to talk with them.

Sharing the gospel with Indian border guards could have got us into trouble. The leader of the trek took a risk. I saw in him what the New Testament calls *parrhesia*—boldness, confidence, openness and freedom of speech. The opposite of *parrhesia* is to be ashamed, to be silent, to be hidden.

This freedom of speech and action was on display in the life of Jesus. Its origin is not human; it is a gift of God. Through the Holy Spirit, Jesus passed on that gift to his disciples, to Paul and to the church in Acts.

Freedom of speech and action is possible because God has

spoken freely in Jesus Christ. He is the Messiah, crucified and risen. He is our only hope of salvation. This Word is alive, active and powerful. It's not about us—our church, our missional community—or about our methods and strategies. It's not about our creative imagination or even about movement pioneers. It's about God and what he has done through Jesus. It's about the power of the Holy Spirit and his dynamic Word. If Jesus died for our sins and rose again, then nothing is too hard for God. He will make a way. The question is, will we join him in this great cause? Will we stare down the giants that confront us every day?

Jesus, living Lord, is the pioneer and perfecter of our faith. Through faith, we are brought into a living union with Christ. The victory is already his.

Movement pioneers have an unshakable faith in the power of God at work through the message of the cross and the resurrection of Jesus Christ. The gospel, as the living Word of God, spreads, grows and multiplies; and wherever it goes, it brings life—new disciples, new churches. Everywhere.

When I share stories like these, I often get the response, "Yes, but that's India. It can happen there. But here it's different. You don't know our context. It won't work here." Okay, it hasn't happened in your context—yet. Why not be the first? That's what movement pioneers do. They go first—until they can say, "Now, there is no place left."

two

Jesus, Our Apostle and Pioneer

*Fix your thoughts on Jesus, whom we
acknowledge as our apostle.*

Hebrews 3:1

Jesus began something completely new in human history—a
missionary movement. Our mission begins and ends with Jesus,
our Apostle. The word *apostle* refers to someone who is *sent*.
Jesus knew he was *sent* by God in a unique way. Forty-one times
in the Gospel of John, Jesus refers to himself as being sent. He
was deeply conscious of being sent with God the Father's authority to speak and act on God's behalf.

Jesus' awareness of being sent flowed from his unique relationship with God as Father and his empowerment by the Spirit.
All four Gospels reveal that both those elements were affirmed
at Jesus' baptism in preparation for the launch of his public ministry. Jesus is the much-loved Son on whom the Spirit has de-
scended (Luke 3:22).

Jesus was *sent* to preach the good news of the kingdom of
God. He was *sent* to the lost sheep of Israel. He was the son of

the vineyard owner *sent* to the rebellious tenants. He was *sent* to give his life as a ransom for many. As the *sent* one, he did not act under his own authority but under the authority of the Father (Luke 4:43; Matthew 15:24; Mark 10:45; 12:1-11; John 17:3, 16).

Jesus' mission was God's mission. He was sent into a hostile world bound by sin and under God's judgment, yet still an object of his love.

John's Gospel stresses how Jesus carried out his mission through obedience and dependence on the Father, who sent him. His mission was to bring glory to the one who sent him. He did not come to do his own will or speak his own words, but to do the will of the one who sent him and speak his words. His works are the works of the one who sent him. Jesus as the Son who was sent sustains an intimate relationship with his Father.[1]

Jesus' death for the world's sins marks the fulfillment of a life obediently submitted to his Father who sent him. His sacrifice and victory make the mission possible. He formed his disciples, who represent every disciple, into the nucleus of a missionary movement. His death and resurrection and the coming of the Spirit mark the beginning of their mission. They have no mission of their own, only his mission. When the risen Lord appeared to his disciples, he told them, "Peace be with you! As the Father has sent me, I am sending you." Then he breathed on them and said, "Receive the Holy Spirit" (John 20:21-22).

Previously the Father was the sender and Jesus was the sent one. Now Jesus is the sender and the disciples are sent. Like Jesus, they are to bring glory to the sender, do the sender's will and make the sender known. They are to know him intimately and follow his example, depending on him in prayer. From now on the disciples are to relate to Jesus the way Jesus related to the Father.[2]

Jesus of Nazareth could only be in one place at one time. Now the limitations of the incarnation are overcome and the gospel will go to all nations through Jesus' disciples. Jesus will be present, through the Holy Spirit, as his disciples fulfill their mission. Jesus' apostolic ministry continues today through his people, who are empowered by the Holy Spirit. It bears his character and his authority, because the risen Lord continues to lead the way.

WHAT DID JESUS DO?

There is no other mission than that of Jesus Christ, God's Son sent to save a lost world through his sacrifice and resurrection. Through the Holy Spirit the exalted Lord Jesus leads the way. To the degree an apostolic ministry continues today, its origin, nature and authority are derived from Jesus Christ. It reflects his mission, his character, his heart.

In *What Jesus Started*, I argued that we must understand Jesus' mission to understand our mission today. What did Jesus do in the Gospels? What did the risen Lord continue to do through his disciples in the book of Acts and the rest of the New Testament? Only as we answer these questions can we ask, What does that look like today?

What Jesus Started identifies six activities that describe what Jesus did as the founder of a missionary movement:

1. *Jesus saw the end.* He focused his ministry on Israel while he prepared his disciples to take the gospel to the whole world.

2. *Jesus connected with people.* Jesus crossed whatever boundaries stood in the way and connected with people who were far from God. He sought people of peace, the people that God had prepared to reach their community.

3. *Jesus shared the gospel.* Jesus called people to repent and believe in the good news. His death brought forgiveness of sins and life with God.

4. *Jesus trained disciples.* Jesus called disciples out from among the crowds. He taught them a new way of life.

5. *Jesus gathered communities.* Jesus' disciples were the nucleus of the renewed people of God. He prepared the way for the birth of the first church at Pentecost. As the risen Lord, Jesus continues to build his church.

6. *Jesus multiplied workers.* Jesus trained his disciples to make disciples and launched a global missionary movement.

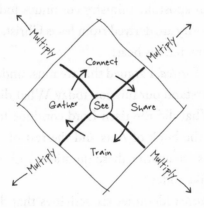

Figure 2.1. Six elements of the movement Jesus started

APOSTLES AND MOVEMENT PIONEERS TODAY

If you hear the word *apostle* and think only of the Twelve and Paul, you'd be mistaken. The New Testament refers to a wide variety of people as apostles. The noun *apostolos* was not a common word in secular Greek, but it appears seventy-nine times in the New Testament, mostly in the writings of Luke and

Paul. The verb *apostellō* means "to send," and frequently "to send with a particular purpose." The noun *apostle* means someone sent with a commission.[3]

Luke records that after a night of prayer Jesus chose twelve out of his wider band of disciples and designated them apostles (Luke 6:12-16). Jesus picked this smaller group "that they might be with him and that he might send them out to preach and to have authority to drive out demons" (Mark 3:13-19). He then sent them out two by two to preach the good news of the kingdom to Israel and to perform signs and wonders. These apostles were to be itinerant and rely on God's provision as they went.

For Jesus, apostleship was far from a static theological concept. During his lifetime the Twelve were appointed to be with him, to learn firsthand from his active engagement in ministry and to share in that ministry. Thus the Twelve are represented in the Gospels as missionaries-in-training. To be an apostle meant to have power and authority to cast out demons, to heal the sick and to preach the gospel of the kingdom. It also meant that one was a representative of Jesus, carrying on his ministry. Apostleship was, for Jesus, a dynamic reality of pioneering ministry.

At the end of the Gospel of Matthew, following the resurrection, Jesus gave his disciples the authority to go into all the world and make disciples of every people group. Jesus further promised to be with them to the end of the age (Matthew 28:19-20). In Luke's account the disciples were instructed to wait in Jerusalem until they were empowered from on high (Luke 24:49).

The Twelve occupy a unique place in God's purposes. Their number is closed, symbolically representing the twelve tribes of the new Israel.[4] Yet the church in a wider sense is apostolic, empowered by the Spirit and sent into the world to continue the ministry of Jesus. The apostolic ministry begun by Jesus continues through his people in the power of the Holy Spirit.[5]

Over one hundred years ago J. B. Lightfoot argued that neither Scripture nor the early Christian writings indicate that apostleship was limited to the Twelve.[6] The New Testament writers apply the term *apostle* to a variety of people other than the Twelve, including Paul and Barnabas (Acts 14:4, 14); James, the brother of Jesus (Galatians 1:19); Apollos (1 Corinthians 4:6-9); Silas and Timothy (1 Thessalonians 1:1; 2:6); Andronicus and Junia (Romans 16:7); and Epaphroditus (Philippians 2:25).[7]

Paul distinguishes the Twelve from "all the apostles" (1 Corinthians 15:5-7). He referred to his opponents at Corinth as "super-apostles" (2 Corinthians 11:5; 12:11) and once as "false apostles" (2 Corinthians 11:13). His problem was not that they called themselves apostles, but that they preached a false gospel.

Paul taught that apostleship is a spiritual gift for the church's common good and ministry (1 Corinthians 12:28-29; Ephesians 4:11-13). In Ephesians 4 Paul lists a variety of leadership functions with the purpose of equipping and maturing the body of Christ. Some of those leadership ministries are more likely to be mobile (apostles, prophets and evangelists) while others are more settled (pastors and teachers). The role of a pastor-teacher is by nature more likely to be limited to a local congregation or network of congregations.[8] Apostles are *sent ones*. The nature of apostolic ministry means it cannot be confined for very long in one location.

Twice Paul places the gift of *apostleship* first on his list of spiritual gifts (1 Corinthians 12:28; Ephesians 4:11). In Ephesians he states that apostles were appointed *first* by God. Why does

Paul list apostles first? An apostle is a pioneer who lays the foundation on which other ministries build. The gift of apostleship has precedence over the other gifts in the founding and building up of the local community of disciples.[9]

The word *apostle* was applied to individuals in the New Testament in two main ways.[10]

1. The band of Jesus' disciples who became known as the Twelve apostles. Jesus formed the Twelve into a missionary band who, as representatives of the whole church, received the command to go into the whole world and make disciples.

The Twelve apostles' uniqueness in the early church, and down through the ages, is as authoritative witnesses of the resurrection and recipients of divine inspiration. They became guardians of the gospel, which is preserved for us in the writings of the New Testament.

The Twelve were, therefore, pioneering leaders and models of apostolic ministry. They were with Jesus in his pioneering ministry, and they laid the foundations for the church in its (Jewish) infancy. Their uniqueness lay not in their function as apostles and pioneers, but in their unique calling as witnesses and guardians of the gospel. The Twelve were apostles par excellence, but they were not the only apostles.

2. A wider group of itinerant missionaries and church planters also known as apostles. Another, wider, group also known as apostles shared the call to go into all the world and make disciples. They were pioneer church planters. However, they did not share the same unique place in God's purposes as witnesses to the resurrection and guardians of apostolic doctrine.

Scripture differentiates between the unique role of the Twelve (and Paul) as the authoritative witnesses to the resurrection and those who functioned as apostles in spreading the gospel, training disciples and multiplying churches. The Twelve and Paul also shared in this functional ministry of apostleship.

The unique role of the Twelve and Paul as authoritative witnesses ended with them and the writing of the New Testament. Yet Jesus continues to call pioneers to lead his people into the fullness of what it means to be a missionary movement.

WHAT DO MOVEMENT PIONEERS DO?

Following the example of Jesus and the first apostles, movement pioneers communicate the truth about the nature of God and salvation through Christ. They teach followers a new way of life in obedience to Christ's commands. Their purpose is to lead people to accept the message, begin to follow Jesus, share him with others and form new communities of faith that become partners in the spread of the gospel.

What does that look like? What do movement pioneers do? They follow the example of Jesus and the disciples he trained.

1. *Movement pioneers see the end.* They obey God's call to join his mission. They submit to the leadership of Jesus through the Holy Spirit and the power of his living Word.

2. *Movement pioneers connect with people.* They cross boundaries (geographic, linguistic, cultural, social, economic) to establish contact with people who are far from God. They seek out responsive people who have been prepared by God.

3. *Movement pioneers share the gospel.* They communicate the truth about the nature of God and salvation through Christ. They equip new disciples to spread the good news throughout their communities.

4. *Movement pioneers train disciples.* They lead people to faith in Jesus Christ (conversion, baptism, gifts of the Holy Spirit) and teach them to obey all that Jesus has commanded.

5. *Movement pioneers gather communities.* They form new believers into church communities featuring the observance of the Lord's Supper, transformation of behavior, love, service and witness.

6. *Movement pioneers multiply workers.* They equip local church leaders to multiply disciples and churches. In partnership with the churches, movement pioneers form apostolic teams that are launched into unreached fields.

Jesus is our apostle; his mission continues today. At the heart of Jesus' mission is the multiplication of disciples and churches— everywhere. That's why the risen Lord continues to call movement pioneers to his cause.

In chapter three we will look at lessons from the life and ministry of the apostle Peter, the first great pioneer of the Christian movement.

three

Peter, First Among the Apostles

For anyone seeking to understand why the church continued to develop and grow beyond the lifetime of its founder, it is worth noting . . . that Jesus entrusted his message and memory not to the whim of anonymous tradition but to named apostolic witnesses who went on to encourage his flock—and to take his gospel to the world.

Markus Bockmuehl, *Simon Peter in Scripture and Memory*

Peter followed Jesus from the beginning. Peter is always listed first among the Twelve. He is their spokesman. Other than Jesus, he is the most frequently mentioned person in the New Testament.[1] After the resurrection Peter was the first of the Twelve to see Jesus. Peter became the first leader of the movement Jesus founded. He was the chosen pioneer of the mission to the Jews and eventually to the Gentiles.[2]

In this sense Peter was first among the apostles, the rock or foundation on which Jesus built his church.[3] He is a pivotal figure in the early Christian movement and a role model as a disciple and as a movement pioneer. The lessons from his life—both good and bad—are meant for our instruction.

THE BOY FROM BETHSAIDA

Sometime between AD 64 and 67, Simon son of Jonah (whom Jesus named Peter) was executed in Rome during Nero's persecution of Christians. Peter was probably in his mid to late sixties. Rome was the fitting place for his death, with its Jewish community of forty to sixty thousand people. Peter was the apostle to the Jews. It was also fitting because Rome was the greatest of all Gentile cities, and Peter was the pioneer of the mission to the Gentiles.

Rome was a long way from Peter's boyhood home of Bethsaida, a northern Galilee fishing town where the Jordan River runs into the Sea of Galilee. Bethsaida was a Jewish town, so Peter grew up speaking Galilean Aramaic. He would also have learned Hebrew in the local synagogue as a boy.

Bethsaida was surrounded by settlements of Greek-speaking Gentiles. Anyone growing up in Bethsaida would have understood some Greek and been familiar with Greek culture and religion. Simon was the Greek name that sounded closest to Peter's Hebrew name, Symeon. His brother Andrew and his friend Philip also went by Greek names.

Before he met Jesus, Peter had moved to nearby Capernaum, a larger fishing village and commercial center. At Capernaum he and Andrew partnered in a fishing business with Zebedee and his sons, James and John. Peter owned his own boat, and the business was large enough to employ workers to help in rowing, handling the sails and heavy nets, and sorting the fish to be ready for market.[4]

A Galilean fisherman lived a hard life under the burden of taxes and charges imposed by Herod Antipas and the nobility. He probably was acquainted with the many tax collectors at Matthew's dinner party with Jesus. They were representatives of Herod.[5]

By the time he settled in Capernaum, Peter was married, living in an extended household with his wife, mother-in-law and his brother Andrew, and probably had children of his own. He had established himself in the world and could provide for his family. Peter had some exposure to Jesus—his teachings, his signs and miracles—but nothing prepared him for the encounter that changed his life and destiny.

MOVEMENT PIONEERS ARE UNQUALIFIED

One day Jesus stepped into Peter's world and shattered it. Jesus was teaching by the shores of the Sea of Galilee. As the crowds pressed in around him, Jesus climbed aboard Peter's boat and asked him to push out from the shore. When Jesus had finished teaching, he told Peter to take his boat out into the lake and throw his nets out for a catch. Peter knew the futility of Jesus' request, but because it was Jesus he obeyed. Immediately, the nets were straining under the weight of a massive catch. Peter, overwhelmed, threw himself at Jesus' feet and cried out, "Go away from me, Lord; I am a sinful man!" (Luke 5:8).

Peter was face to face with the presence of God in the person of Jesus, and he was helpless and unworthy. Jesus called Peter to follow him and promised to teach him to fish for people. Peter, together with his brother Andrew, James and John, left everything and followed Jesus. This encounter on the lake was both Peter's conversion and his call.

The Gospel writers don't explain why Jesus chose Peter. Their focus is not on Peter's qualities or shortcomings, but on the authority of Jesus to call and to equip Peter for the task.

Without Jesus' intervention in Peter's life, we would never have heard of him. Every significant breakthrough in Peter's development as a movement pioneer was initiated by God: the miraculous catch of fish, the call to follow Jesus and learn how to fish for people, the revelation at the Transfiguration, the confession that Jesus is the Messiah at Caesarea. Even Peter's sifting by Satan was not outside of God's control. The restoration by the risen Christ, the coming of the Holy Spirit, the mission to the Jews and Gentiles, rescue from persecution, even his imprisonment and death were ordained by God. The initiative is always with God.

Peter is the one person who experienced the outpouring of the Holy Spirit at three critical turning points in the spread of the gospel. He was there when the Spirit came upon (1) Jewish believers at Pentecost, then (2) in Samaria and finally (3) at the house of Cornelius, when the Spirit came upon the Gentiles.

By the power of the Holy Spirit, Peter healed in the name of Jesus, freed those tormented by evil spirits, preached the gospel and confronted the same religious leaders who had crucified Jesus. By God's power Peter rebuked Simon the sorcerer, escaped from jail, endured threats and beatings, raised Dorcas back to life and took the gospel to the Gentiles.

Peter was not a self-made man. When the religious leaders of Jerusalem saw Peter's boldness, they were amazed when they realized he was an uneducated amateur. He was unqualified except for one characteristic—he had been with Jesus.[6]

MOVEMENT PIONEERS LEARN AS THEY GO

Peter learned by watching what Jesus did. He learned Jesus' way of life, his teaching and his methods. One night the whole town of Capernaum gathered outside Peter's home, where Jesus was staying, while Jesus healed the sick and cast out demons.[7] He too learned to heal the sick, cast out demons and teach what Jesus taught.

Peter's settled life was disrupted as he traveled with Jesus to every town and village in Galilee—all 175 of them (Matthew 9:35).[8] There were also mission trips south into Judea and to Jerusalem. Jesus sent his disciples out in pairs with no other support than faith in God (Luke 10:1-24). They expected that if an unreached town was receptive, someone would invite them in and provide food and lodging. If that didn't happen, these leaders in training went without food and shelter. Peter learned that a God-prepared insider is the key to reaching whole communities.[9]

As they traveled from town to town on mission, Jesus trained Peter's head, heart and hands. His classroom was on the road, in the marketplace, by the lake, at a meal, in a garden, in an empty tomb. At Pentecost, Peter became the leader of the movement Jesus started. Peter didn't always get it right, but when he did, it was because he had been with Jesus.

Peter followed Jesus' example and developed leaders around him on the go. In the early years Peter often had John at his side—when he healed a lame man, when he proclaimed the gospel and when he was imprisoned (Acts 3–4). As the movement grew in size and complexity, Peter and the Twelve created leadership positions for seven representatives of the Greek-speaking Jewish believers. These men were appointed to settle a problem with the distribution of food to Greek-speaking widows, but they were soon taking the lead in spreading the gospel (Acts 6). Stephen paid with his life for his proclamation of the gospel (Acts 7). Philip, without any sanction from Peter or the apostles, was led by God to take the gospel to the Samaritans (Acts 8). The movement spread by the leading and power of the Holy Spirit without central planning and control by the apostles. Peter and John later went to Samaria, supported Philip's pioneering mission and added their own momentum to it by preaching extensively in Samaritan towns.

Peter took other disciples with him on mission. When God called him to take the gospel to Cornelius and his friends and family, Peter took six other disciples with him and had them, not him, baptize the new believers (Acts 10:45-48; cf. Acts 11:12).

Peter shared ministry with others, and he supported the work of others. He developed leaders who took responsibility for the church in Jerusalem and moved on to unreached regions. When Peter's job was done in Jerusalem, there was a transition of leadership from Peter and the Twelve to James (brother of Jesus) and the elders. Peter and the apostles were the most prominent leaders of the Jerusalem church in its early years. During that time they prepared James and the elders to step into the leadership of the local churches in and around the city.

MOVEMENT PIONEERS LIVE THE GOSPEL

The high point of Peter's early discipleship with Jesus was the Mount of Transfiguration (Luke 9:28-36). On that mountain, when Peter caught a glimpse of Jesus' divinity, he did not know what to say, but he spoke anyway, "Master, it is good for us to be here. Let us put up three shelters—one for you, one for Moses and one for Elijah."

The cloud of God's awesome presence surrounded Peter, James and John. They fell to the ground overcome by fear. God declared, "This is my Son, whom I have chosen; listen to him."

When the voice had spoken and the cloud had lifted, Peter saw Jesus standing alone. Jesus then took the men back down the mountain and soon "resolutely set out" to go to Jerusalem (Luke 9:51), where he would suffer and die a shameful death.

Peter could not accept that the Messiah must die a shameful death, cursed by God and deserted by his closest companions. He could not accept a suffering Messiah who came to serve and to give his life as a ransom for many.

Jesus knew this. He knew that Satan would sift Peter like wheat. Jesus knew Peter's faith would fail, so he prayed for Peter and urged him to turn again to God and become the rock who strengthens his brothers (Luke 22:31-32). Jesus knew that Peter would never grasp the reality of God's grace until he had faced the reality of his sinfulness. Only then would he become a rock on which Jesus would build the restored people of God.

The message Peter now boldly proclaimed at Pentecost was not his gospel. Without the crucified and risen Lord, without the power of the Holy Spirit, there was no message, no movement. Peter preached the first missionary message in Jerusalem to the pilgrims gathered from around the world. He told them the last days had begun; the restoration of Israel had begun. The Spirit had been poured out as promised by the prophet Joel. Now was the time to repent.

When the crowd cried, "What shall we do?" Peter replied, "Repent and be baptized, every one of you, in the name of Jesus Christ for the forgiveness of your sins. And you will receive the gift of the Holy Spirit" (Acts 2:37-38).

From the moment they first met, Jesus had been writing the gospel on Peter's heart. Now on the other side of Easter, Peter understood and proclaimed it with power and authority.

MOVEMENT PIONEERS STAY ON TARGET

Soon after the heights of Pentecost, Peter faced a down-to-earth problem—conflict among God's people. There was a daily distribution of food to impoverished widows among the believers in Jerusalem. Many of these widows had settled in the holy city after living in the Jewish Diaspora among the Gentiles. They spoke only Greek, and their needs had been overlooked.

Peter and the apostles appointed leaders with a Greek-speaking background who could resolve the problem. Yet the apostles would not neglect their primary calling—prayer and the ministry of the word (Acts 6:1-4). To our ears "prayer and the ministry of the word" sounds like something a pastor does in his study before preaching to the faithful on Sundays. Yet almost every message recorded in Acts is an evangelistic message in a missionary setting.[10]

The Word is a living force unleashed by the living God (Acts 4:4, 29, 31). The success of the mission was not due to Peter or any of the apostles, but to the power of God through his dynamic Word (Acts 6:2-4, 7).

The prayers recorded are for the advance of the gospel in the face of persecution (see Acts 4:23-30). So when the apostles described their priority as "prayer and the ministry of the word," it meant they were leaders of an expanding missionary movement driven by the living Word and the power of God released through prayer.

Following Pentecost Peter was based in Jerusalem, a city of one hundred thousand permanent residents and the center of the world for the Jewish Diaspora. Jerusalem drew hundreds of thousands of pilgrims every year. Thousands of Diaspora Jews, like the young Saul and his family, settled in Jerusalem and maintained their contacts with friends and family in the cities of the

Roman and Persian empires. Many of those who heard Peter's Pentecost message returned home to spread that message in faraway places. Over the next twelve years, while Peter was based in Jerusalem, the pilgrims continued to visit the city and heard the gospel.[11]

Luke tells us that every day, in the temple and from house to house, the believers did not cease teaching and preaching Jesus as the Christ (Acts 5:42). People brought their sick from the neighboring towns and villages around Jerusalem to be healed by Peter and others, just as the people of Capernaum had once gathered outside Peter's door to be healed by Jesus. The movement in and around Jerusalem grew by thousands.

Peter and the disciples proclaimed the message of salvation on the Temple Mount, in the synagogues and from house to house. They were motivated by the conviction that there was salvation in no other name than Jesus (Acts 4:12).[12]

The same religious leaders who opposed Jesus also opposed Peter. They accused Peter and the apostles of filling Jerusalem with Jesus' teaching (Acts 5:28). Peter overcame his fear and endured threats, beatings and imprisonment with boldness and conviction.

Luke tells us that the church grew in strength, and, living in the fear of the Lord and encouraged by the Holy Spirit, it increased in numbers (Acts 9:31). Under Peter's leadership, the churches spread throughout Jerusalem, Judea, Galilee and Samaria, and on the coastal plain to the west—in Lydda, Joppa, Caesarea, Ptolemais and maybe Ashdod (see fig. 3.1).

Peter was not the pastor of these churches but an apostle commissioned by Jesus to reach Jews and Gentiles.[13] Through a ministry focused on prayer and the Word, Peter multiplied and strengthened disciples and church communities wherever he went.

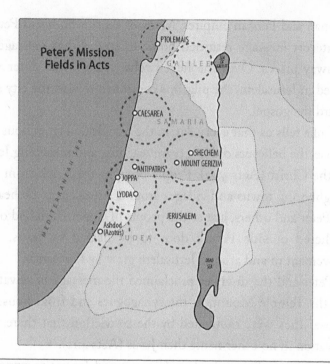

Figure 3.1. Like Jesus' ministry, Peter's ministry could not be contained to one group of people in one location.

MOVEMENT PIONEERS WON'T BE FENCED IN

Peter's ministry was never confined to one location. Oscar Cullmann observes the irony that "the apostle who later is regarded as the personification of organized church government in reality exercised such a function for only a short time in the beginning, and then exchanged it for missionary work."[14] Jerusalem was Peter's base for missions into Samaria, Judea, Galilee, the cities of the coastal plain and Caesarea. His mission was to Jews, Samaritans and Gentiles. Jesus had taught him how to enter an unreached region without any resources, find responsive people and leave behind the nucleus of a new community of disciples.

Back in Jerusalem, James, Jesus' brother, together with the elders, emerged as the leader of the church. For a time there was an overlap of leadership while Peter and the Twelve were based in Jerusalem. Then in AD 41 Herod Agrippa I unleashed another wave of persecution. He arrested the apostle James and executed him, and threw Peter in jail, intending to kill him too.

God had other plans and arranged a miraculous escape. Peter left for "another place" (Acts 12:17). He had to escape Herod's jurisdiction, which meant leaving Judea, Galilee and Samaria. Jerusalem no longer served as the base for Peter's pioneering ministry. From that time James, the brother of Jesus, and the elders, not the apostles, led the church in Jerusalem. Peter had left Jerusalem to pursue his mission to the Jews and Gentiles beyond Israel.

The twelve apostles were not primarily organizers or coordinators of the work of the church. They were movement pioneers. Once the churches in Jerusalem, Judea, Galilee and Samaria— with thousands of believers—were consolidated, the apostles handed over the leadership.[15]

We are not told where Peter went. The author of Acts has other concerns. Luke assumes his readers know about the pioneering ministry of Peter and his wife (1 Corinthians 9:5; Galatians 2:11-14). Early traditions point to the northern regions of Asia Minor (modern-day Turkey) as one of Peter's mission fields. His first letter is addressed to the believers in Asia Minor—those from Pontus, Galatia, Cappadocia, Asia and Bithynia. These churches may have been the fruit of his mission. Peter could also have traveled to the larger Jewish communities of Antioch in Syria, Alexandria in Egypt and Ephesus in Asia. There is a strong tradition that by the mid-60s AD, at the end of his life,

Peter was in Rome, the capital of the empire, which had a population of around one million people (see fig. 3.2).

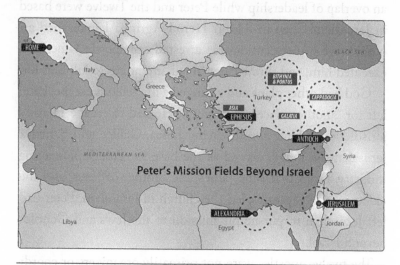

Figure 3.2. Peter's mission fields beyond Israel

Peter returned to Jerusalem briefly in AD 48 to attend the Jerusalem Council. James, the Lord's brother, led the discussions, not Peter. At the council Peter was the pivotal figure who bridged the divide between the Jewish and Gentile missions. Through his example with Cornelius the Gentiles were accepted as full members of the body of Christ without the requirement that they come under the Jewish law.

Peter, not Paul, was the first missionary to the Gentiles. His bridging leadership ensured that the way was now clear for Paul and others to take the gospel to the ends of the earth.

MOVEMENT PIONEERS ARE LIKE JESUS IN LIFE AND DEATH

Like the great apostle Paul, Peter was not competent to fulfill his apostolic task. Jesus called, equipped and rescued him from defeat and failure. He taught him what to say and do. He filled him with the Holy Spirit. The dynamic word of the gospel did the rest. The result was a multiplying movement of disciples and churches.

It's most likely that Emperor Nero had Peter executed. The fisherman did not have the same social status and rights of Paul, a Roman citizen, who was probably beheaded. According to tradition, Nero ordered Peter crucified. Peter had become like Jesus in life and in death. He remains today an example of a movement pioneer who stood strong to the end.

PIONEER PROFILE

Hudson Taylor and the Second Era
of Protestant Missions

No other one organization, Roman Catholic or
Protestant, sent so many missionaries to China or was
found in so many provinces. In no other land of so large an
area and population was there ever a single society which
planned so comprehensively to cover the whole and
came so near to fulfilling its dream.

Kenneth Scott Latourette,
A History of the Expansion of Christianity

The first era of Protestant missions began in 1792 when William Carey published his missionary manifesto and formed the Baptist Missionary Society. The following year he arrived in India as the Society's first missionary. Others followed his example, and the Protestant missionary movement was born. With the manifesto and the Society, Protestants had both the motivation and the means to fulfill the Great Commission.

In this first era the focus was reaching the relatively accessible coastlands of Asia and Africa. Opening up the interior was the focus of the second era.[1]

In 1853 a small clipper sailed out of Liverpool, England, with a twenty-one-year-old missionary on board. Hudson Taylor was bound for China. It was the unlikely beginning of a new era in Protestant world missions. Through this movement pioneer the focus would shift from the coastlands, where most missionaries lived, to the unreached interior. To meet the challenge of this new frontier the faith-mission movement was born through this chronically ill, frequently depressed young man from Yorkshire.

Before his birth Taylor's father had knelt beside his pregnant mother and prayed, "Dear God, if you should give us a son, grant that he may work for you in China." Six months after the ship left Liverpool, it sailed into Shanghai, one of five ports under the Treaty of Nanking in which foreigners were allowed to live. Hudson Taylor arrived in China to serve with the Chinese Evangelization Society.

Only seven of China's eighteen provinces had missionaries. Most of them were concentrated in a few coastal cities. Taylor began making long journeys into the interior. As a Westerner he stood out and at times attracted violent opposition. So he wore Chinese clothes, adopted local customs and grew a pigtail. His behavior shocked other missionaries. Taylor was equally offended by their worldliness. They preferred the relative safety and comfort of Shanghai, where English businessmen and diplomats needed them as translators.

Taylor's mission agency proved to be incompetent. In 1857 Taylor became an independent missionary. He refused to ask family and friends for money, and depended on God alone for his needs. He left Shanghai for Ningpo, where he planted a small church. There he met and married twenty-year-old Maria Dyer. Maria had been born in China of missionary parents who had since died. Their match was opposed by other missionaries who were unimpressed by Hudson Taylor and his methods.

When in 1860 what may have been hepatitis forced Taylor to return to England, it looked like they might never see China again. But Hudson Taylor could not forget China. He hung a large map of China on the wall of his study and placed pins in the seventy locations where he knew Protestant missionaries were working. As he lay recuperating he kept returning to the map to pray and to think. One day he realized what should have been obvious—most of the pins were on the coast, very few in the interior. The map became his "accusing map."

Hudson Taylor believed that the Chinese people were lost without Christ. He believed that the church was charged by Christ to "go into all the world and make disciples." He felt the weight of responsibility for the millions of Chinese who were dying without Christ. Yet he was equally troubled by the burden of sending young men and women into the interior of China to face sickness and persecution—dangers he knew firsthand.

He had no doubt that as he prayed God would provide the workers and the funds. But could he trust God to sustain him as their leader? He was troubled and torn for months. A friend who was concerned invited him to Brighton on the south coast of England for a weekend break. After worship on Sunday morning he was "unable to bear the sight of a congregation of a thousand or more Christian people rejoicing in their own security while millions were perishing for lack of knowledge."[2] He wrote, "I wandered out on the sands alone, in great spiritual agony."

Then on that Brighton beach God met him: "There the Lord conquered my unbelief, and I surrendered myself to God for this service. I told him that all responsibility as to the issues and consequences must rest with him; that as his servant it was mine to obey and to follow him—his to direct, to care for, and to guide me and those who might labor with me."

In that same year, with Maria's help, he wrote and published *China's Spiritual Needs and Claims*. By his calculation a million Chinese were dying without Christ every month. Someone needed to send workers beyond the five treaty ports deep into the interior of China. As no agency was willing to do that, Taylor formed his own—the China Inland Mission (CIM), the first of what became known as faith missions. It could equally be described as the beginning of the frontier mission movement.[3] In the days of William Carey, everywhere outside the Western world was a frontier. Now the frontier had shifted from the accessible coastal areas to the interior of places like China and Africa.

This new mission agency would be shaped by six principles: (1) China Inland Mission would accept missionaries from any denomination, if they could sign a simple statement of belief. (2) CIM would accept candidates who were "willing and skillful workers" despite any lack of formal education. (3) Authority was in the hands of field leadership, not a distant board in England. (4) Missionaries would adopt Chinese dress and customs. (5) They would not ask for money. Workers did not receive a set salary but trusted God to provide. (6) Their purpose was widespread evangelism in the interior of China, where Christ had not been preached.[4]

Taylor specifically asked for twenty-four missionaries. Two for each of China's eleven provinces without a missionary, and two for Mongolia. The response was dramatic as young men and women volunteered for China.

Less than a year later, in 1866, when the clipper Lammermuir sailed out of the East India dock in London, on board were Hudson and Maria Taylor, their four children and sixteen young recruits—six men and ten women. They were headed to China to join the five CIM missionaries already working there.

Most CIM missionaries were from humble backgrounds and had little formal education. The exceptions were the Cambridge Seven, who gave up wealth and privilege to go to China. Many of the workers were women, and Taylor was condemned by other mission agencies for allowing single women to serve in the interior.

Progress came at a price. Idealism and faith were tested by pressures of life in a strange culture, in remote locations. Conflict over Taylor's methods and leadership took a toll. Some left the mission; others were asked to leave. They faced sickness, danger and persecution.

Taylor's methods and leadership were attacked from within CIM and by other missionaries. He suffered from depression, constant poor health and a spinal injury that almost crippled him. Four of their eight children died before they reached ten. In 1870 Maria, pregnant, became seriously ill. She gave birth to a boy who lived just two weeks. A few days after his death Maria died. She was thirty-three.

Despite the heartache and the opposition, Taylor was resolute. He wrote, "China is not to be won for Christ by quiet, ease-loving men and women." He wanted men and women who would put Jesus, China and souls first in everything—even life itself must be secondary.[5]

By 1870 there were thirty-nine adults in twenty-one locations in four provinces. In 1875 he asked for eighteen more workers. The prayer was answered. In 1881 he prayed for another seventy missionaries by the end of 1884, and he received seventy-six. In 1886 he asked for one hundred, and by the end of 1887 he had 102, and the funds to get them to China.[6]

Evangelism was the priority of CIM, but church planting was the fruit of making disciples. Through his friendship with John Nevius Taylor, he became committed to planting indigenous churches that were self-supporting, self-governing and self-propagating. By 1890 CIM had eighty churches with three thousand baptized converts.[7]

In 1891 CIM had 641 foreign workers and 462 Chinese workers serving in 260 locations. There were workers in all but three provinces of China, including the remote regions of Xinjiang and the border region with Tibet.

Taylor showed that residential mission work was possible throughout China. The mission agencies that had opposed his methods began following his example. New faith missions that followed the example of the Hudson Taylor and CIM sprang up in Europe and the English-speaking world.

But the most painful blow of all came in the summer of 1900. Taylor was recovering in Switzerland from physical and emotional collapse when the Boxer Rebellion broke out in China. Fifty-eight of his workers and twenty-one of their children were murdered.

Five years later Hudson Taylor died on his last visit to China. He was buried beside Maria in Zhenjiang next to the Yangtze River. By that time 825 CIM missionaries were working in every province of China. They had seen 18,000 Chinese converted. In 1914 the China Inland Mission became the largest mission agency in the world.

four

Structuring for Movements

*There is no hint that Luke takes the so-called apostolic
age as somehow totally unique and unrepeatable.*

Ben Witherington III,
The Acts of the Apostles

Jesus unleashed something totally new in human history—a
missionary movement that had the whole world in its sights.
The advance began at Pentecost and continued for the next
three hundred years until millions throughout Europe, the
Middle East, Asia and Africa confessed Christ as Lord.[1] Never
has any movement—social, religious or political—achieved
such a rapid advance in a dominant culture without the aid of
military force.

The book of Acts gave every indication that apostolic ministry
would continue beyond the first generation of the Christian
movement. Therefore we should expect to find that movement
pioneers keep popping up throughout history.

THE RISE OF MONASTICISM

The conversion of the Roman emperor Constantine in AD 312

led to an increasing flood of people into the Christian church, so much so that by the end of the fifth century the overwhelming majority of people in the Roman Empire identified themselves as Christians. The church enjoyed an increasingly privileged position in society. However, power, wealth and respectability brought moral and spiritual decline.[2]

"The rise of monasticism was, after Christ's commission to his disciples, the most important—and in many ways the most beneficial—institutional event in the history of Christianity," observes Mark Noll.[3] Monasticism was a people's movement formed in reaction to that decline. At first the bishops and clergy opposed the movement. Yet, for over a thousand years, the history of Christian mission is the history of monasticism.[4] The origins of Christian monasticism lie in the fourth century in the deserts of Egypt and Syria.

The early pioneer of monasticism was a twenty-year-old Egyptian named Anthony. Around AD 270, when his parents died, Anthony gave his possessions to the poor and lived a solitary, ascetic life. His example inspired others. As he withdrew further and further into the desert he was followed by disciples eager to learn from his example. The monks lived alone in their huts or caves, spending their days seeking union with God. When they weren't praying, they worked with their hands, gathering weekly for worship and prayer.

In about AD 320 a former soldier named Pachomius organized the monks into communities living under a written rule of life. Monasticism was born as a movement. Over time the monastic movement emerged as a missionary force. While the church made its peace with the world, the monastic movement became a magnet for dedicated followers of Christ. The ideas and practices of the desert fathers profoundly influenced Columba and his successors.

MONASTICISM ABANDONED

The Reformers rejected monasticism as a corrupt institution that created two classes of believers. They abolished the religious orders in the territories they controlled without replacing them with a functional equivalent.

In the sixteenth century, Roman Catholic missions were at their peak, yet Protestants made almost no attempt to spread the gospel beyond the borders of Europe. C. W. Ranson notes, "The paradox of the Protestantism of the Reformation era is that while it called the Church back to its apostolic faith it was largely content to leave the fulfillment of the apostolic mission to the Church of Rome."[5] Some Reformers argued that the Great Commission ceased with the apostles. Others believed that the ministry of apostolic pioneers ceased once churches were established. Mission was no longer crossing cultural and geographic boundaries with the gospel, but fulfilling one's calling in everyday life. Mobile missionary bands were no longer required. Every Christian had his own parish and each bishop his diocese, and no one could claim a roving commission. The call of every believer to fulfill the Great Commission was viewed as subversive to the social order.

Thus, Protestants had no vision or means to carry out world missions for over 250 years, until William Carey and the emergence of Protestant missionary societies. Regarding this sad fact, Arthur Glasser comments, "Only when there are no more frontiers to be crossed—only when Jesus Christ has returned and subdued all peoples under his authority—will it be possible to say that the need for such missionary bands has finally come to an end."[6]

In my university days I met a campus worker from a parachurch organization. He tried to convince me that most people in local churches were deadwood. He believed they were not serious about their faith or committed to making disciples. So he didn't waste his time going to church. The problem with his thinking is that the New Testament has no categories for a disciple who is not grounded in a local church. Followers of Jesus participate in church life as the New Testament understands church.

Some people make the opposite error and regard mission agencies as God's second best, a necessary evil. God's plan A is to work only through the local church. But when churches don't do their job, God resorts to plan B and works through mission agencies and parachurch groups. Mission agencies are God's second best.

This view ignores the New Testament pattern of missionary bands reflected in Jesus' ministry and in the examples of Peter and Paul. We also have the witness of history, which shows that breakthroughs into new unreached fields are rarely (not never) done without some form of mission structure.[7]

So, how are we to understand the relationship between movement pioneers, their teams and the local churches? Who's in charge? What are their respective functions? How do they partner in mission? Or are they independent of each other?

MISSION BAND AND LOCAL CHURCH

Barnabas and Paul's call to leave Antioch (Acts 13:1-4) is an example of the emergence of a missionary band out of a local church. From the account we see that both the mobile apostolic band and the local church are legitimate expressions of God's mission. The resulting apostolic band had its own identity and existence apart from the local expression of the body of Christ. The missionary band received funds and personnel from the churches but operated independently of their control.[8] Paul's missionary enterprise was not under the authority and direction of the church at Antioch or in Jerusalem or any other church.

Paul did not seek to rule over the churches. Paul encouraged churches to grow to maturity without depending on him to lead them. He wanted the churches to become full partners in support of his pioneering ministry.

The Christian movement has two structures: the local church and the missionary band. A local congregation is composed of anyone who is a follower of Jesus Christ. Joining a missionary band requires a second commitment to the task of the missionary band.[9]

The demanding nature of pioneering ministry requires a different structure from the local church. Paul did not expect every believer to join his apostolic band. He expected local churches to participate in mission locally and partner with his mission beyond. He called workers out of the local churches to join his apostolic band for varying lengths of time.

The history of the Christian movement reveals that breakthroughs in the spread of the gospel into unreached fields normally require focused mission structures. These mission structures begin on the fringe, not at the ecclesiastical center. Unrecognized groups of ordinary people with little or no status in the church have started at least half of the mission movements in the history of the church.[10] The expansion of the church has always been carried on most effectively when these two structures have accepted each other's legitimacy and worked in partnership.

I believe the New Testament shows that both the missionary band and the local church are ordained by God. Some go further and describe both entities as *church*. Can we call the missionary band a *church*? I don't think so. The New Testament never refers to Paul and his coworkers as a *church*. The local church by its nature is open to all who believe, while a missionary band is restricted to a few.[11] There are good reasons for not calling mission bands churches, as though somehow they are a functional equivalent to the local church. Yet the closest possible relationship exists between the missionary band and the local church.

Nevertheless, when Paul and his team traveled to a location, they immediately formed a church. They would have worshiped, celebrated the Lord's Supper and gathered to hear and obey the Word. They would have loved one another and given generously. How could they not be the church? Missionaries do not leave the church behind when they enter a new field.[12]

If mission agencies were churches, they could conclude, "Our people don't need to participate in or plant local churches. We are already a self-contained church." Paul's team existed only to form new churches in unreached areas. His team was not an end in itself. It was not a self-contained entity that existed apart from planting and strengthening local churches. Paul never called his team a *church* because the missionary band was not the goal of their mission. The goal of his apostolic ministry was a new church in an unreached field. The team existed as both a missionary band and a local church in formation. When new disciples were made, they were gathered into the church. But only a few ever joined Paul's mobile missionary band.

Paul's apostolic band was an expression of the body of Christ in mission, not an end in itself. It was the seed for a new church or churches in a region. The danger of calling mission structures churches is that they may lose sight of their unique mandates. They do not exist to be a church; they exist to form new local churches in which team members participate. Apostolic ministry does not elevate individuals out of the local body of Christ.

Once local churches are established, pioneers begin looking for new, unreached fields. The churches continue the spread of the gospel in depth. This includes planting new churches in their regions. The churches also send out workers to take the gospel beyond their local areas. The Great Commission is the responsibility of every disciple, every local church and every missionary band.

THE CREATIVE TENSION OF PARTNERSHIP

There are two equal and opposite errors in structuring the relationship between the churches and the missionary bands. On one side, one party attempts to dominate or control the other. On the other side, one party or both seek to be independent. The solution to these extremes is an interdependent relationship expressed in partnership for mission.

Control. Control takes place when one party directs the activities of the other. Typically, this happens when local churches

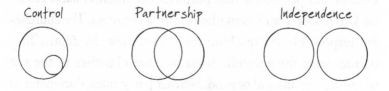

Figure 4.1. Models for mission band and local church relationship

or denominations seek to control the activity of the apostolic bands. Control can be exercised because the churches have the resources and people that the apostolic band needs to fulfill its mission. When this imbalance occurs, local churches and denominations seek to rein in the work of movement pioneers rather than release resources and people for reaching new fields.

When movement pioneers seek to control the churches, the opposite imbalance produces the same result. Mission leaders settle down to care for local churches rather than opening up new fields. Circuit riders were the early pioneers of Methodism. They were mobile evangelists and church planters responsible to reach a region rather than settle in one location. They equipped local Methodists to lead a growing network of churches. Eventually, when they got off their horses and became settled pastors of local churches, the Methodist movement lost its momentum.[13]

Partnership. Paul resisted the pressure to settle down as the pastor of the churches he planted. He worked to develop local leaders and mature churches that no longer depended on him but could support his mission into new fields with prayer, workers and giving. Paul wanted partnership with the churches.

Partnership occurs when local churches and apostolic bands affirm the legitimacy and unique contributions of the other. The pioneers seek out unreached fields. The churches release resources and people for that purpose. The mission band circles back to report to and strengthen existing churches. The churches are responsible for reaching their local areas in depth. They partner with the apostolic band to plant churches in the surrounding regions and beyond. Neither party rules, dominates or controls the other.

Independence. Independence occurs when at least one party breaks away from the relationship. Typically, this happens when the mission agency or apostolic band regards local church membership as a second-rate alternative to committed discipleship. They need the church's financial support and people, but deep down they regard the church as a second-best option for making disciples. They make "disciples" without planting churches, a concept that is totally foreign to the Scriptures.

Churches become independent from apostolic ministry when they refuse to reach out beyond their local areas and existing ministries. They lack the expertise, structures and willingness to release people and resources to multiply beyond their borders. They regard the mission structures as illegitimate and a threat to their authority and control of their people.

GUIDING PRINCIPLES FOR MISSIONARY BAND–CHURCH PARTNERSHIPS

In summary, these are the principles that guide a beneficial relationship between the apostolic band and the local church.

1. God remains responsible for his mission and, through the Word and the Spirit, empowers and directs his people to participate in it.

2. The spread of the gospel is at the heart of God's mission, resulting in the multiplication of disciples and churches.

3. There are two structures for the fulfillment of God's mission—local churches and apostolic bands.

4. Churches are responsible for reaching their regions in depth. They are also responsible to partner with pioneers in taking the gospel to unreached fields beyond their geography or cultures.

5. Apostolic bands are responsible, in partnership with the churches, to spread the gospel in fields that are unreached geographically or culturally. They spread the gospel, make disciples, and multiply and strengthen churches.

6. Both structures are self-governing under the leading of the Holy Spirit and the authority of the Word. Neither controls, directs nor dominates the other.

7. Partnership is the relationship God intends between the churches and the apostolic bands.

John Howard Schutz observes, "Both the Church and the apostle are to be subordinate to and manifestations of the one gospel."[14]

The Contrast

Church	Band
local	mobile
mission in depth	mission in breadth
long term	pioneering
self-governing	self-governing

The Partnership

Church	Band
release money, workers and prayer	rely on the churches for support
mission in depth	return, report in
long term	train local leaders, mobilize for local mission
self-governing	strengthen existing churches

Figure 4.2. Church and missionary band: contrast and partnership

MOVE: A CASE STUDY

What could this look like in practice? The example I know best is MOVE (movenetwork.org), the mission agency I lead together with my wife, Michelle. MOVE—formerly Church Resource Ministries Australia (CRM)—was founded in 1988 to serve churches in leadership development, church health and church planting. We provided resources, training and coaching to church leaders. In 2012, we changed our name from CRM to MOVE to reflect a major shift in the movements paradigm. We reoriented our mission around multiplying disciples and churches—everywhere. Whether our workers are in Bangkok, Sydney, London, Mysore or Honiara, we connect with lost people, share the gospel, train disciples, gather communities and multiply workers. We know what this looks like day by day.

We pursue our mission in close partnership with local churches. All of our workers are supported through prayer, giving and encouragement by local churches and individual believers. We regard the world as our mission field, including our home base of Australia. We have workers in Australia who do what missionaries do—make disciples and plant churches. We also partner with local churches to train them to do the same. We are just as committed to fueling church-planting movements in Australia as we are in India.

Whether we're in India or Australia, we model effective ministry and train and partner with local churches to mobilize the whole body of Christ for mission. As we train, we look for those who are faithful and fruitful and help them become multipliers.

As churches are planted, they never become MOVE churches. Our workers never become local church pastors. To do that would be to blur the distinction between the local church and the mission band. The churches make their own decisions regarding which formal or informal associations they join. They may join an existing network or denomination, or form new networks.

Our goal is to develop local leaders who take responsibility, under God, for the health and multiplication of new churches. We work toward multiple streams of fourth generational churches. Those are churches who typically produce up to four generations of new churches.

We look for movement pioneers to emerge from the churches. We partner with those churches and movement pioneers to take the gospel to unreached fields. Typically, in overseas fields, we do not recruit those pioneers into our organization. We prefer to help them set up their own missionary bands as an equal partner with MOVE. In developing nations we do not pay local people to plant or pastor churches, but we help with the cost of training. We encourage proven multipliers to raise support locally.

MOVE is just one example of a new wave of mission agencies solely committed to multiplying disciples and churches in partnership with existing churches.

A sign of life. A clear sign of the vitality of the Christian movement is the birth of new movements for the renewal and expansion of the Christian faith. That is why the New Testament devotes so many pages to the story of the spread of the gospel through mobile apostolic bands in partnership with local churches. The advance of the Christian movement has always depended on a healthy partnership between these bands and local churches. That partnership should be characterized by interdependence rather than control or independence.

five
. . . .

No Place Left in South Asia

There is no more place for me to work in these regions.

Romans 15:23

In 1996 Sam Beckdahl lay dying. His children and grand-children were gathered around his bedside keeping vigil. Among them was his grandson Nathan Shank. When Grandpa Beckdahl had breathed his last, they joined hands as Nathan's great-uncle prayed, "Lord, receive his spirit."[1]

Nathan opened his eyes and lifted his head. His grandmother looked straight at him and said, "The burden has passed to you!" That burden was God's missionary call to north India. Nathan's family tree showed generations of missionaries. Two sets of great-grandparents served on the India-Nepal border during the British colonial rule one hundred years ago. Nathan's grand-parents were born in India and served there as missionaries. Many of his great-uncles and aunts were missionaries.

What would they have thought if they could have seen him at his grandfather's bedside—a young adult going through the motions of attending college, far from God, wandering through life looking for the next party?

Nathan's grandmother's words meant little to him at the time. Nathan was not in a place to hear from God. But her words stayed with him. Within twelve months, he had returned to faith in Christ. God confirmed his call on Nathan's life through the apostle Paul's charge to Timothy:

> In the presence of God and of Christ Jesus, who will judge the living and the dead, and in view of his appearing and his kingdom, I give you this charge: Preach the word; be prepared in season and out of season; correct, rebuke and encourage—with great patience and careful instruction. (2 Timothy 4:1-2)

Nathan graduated from college with a degree in education and applied to go to Nepal with a mission agency.

Following some basic training, Nathan arrived in Nepal in August 2000. He threw himself into language study and fieldwork. He was the evangelist, the disciple maker and the church planter. He worked hard, and within two years he and two partners had planted three churches.

Despite his initial success, Nathan despaired when he compared his efforts with the challenge of reaching the region of north India and Nepal. He realized he was never going to get the job done.

In his last year in Nepal, the Lord introduced Nathan to a young lady who was involved in a short-term mission. Kari had come to faith only months before her arrival in Nepal. It soon became obvious to both Nathan and Kari that God had called them to walk together in marriage and mission.

When Nathan returned to the United States, he and Kari were married and began theological studies together. They worked hard and graduated from seminary in the spring of 2005. During those years, Nathan was troubled by the gap between what his best efforts on the field could produce and the need in South Asia. He knew something had to be different but was uncertain how to proceed.

As Nathan returned to South Asia, he recognized the Lord was expanding his vision beyond Nepal to include the north Indian Hindi-speaking belt and the neighboring country of Bhutan. This expanded vision included more than 400 million lost people. Nathan pressed forward, confident the Lord had led him to claim these areas and diverse populations for the kingdom.

Looking back, Nathan felt that the biggest barrier to a church-planting movement in north India and Nepal had been Nathan Shank. He realized he had too much faith in his own abilities. They had blinded him to the power of God and the resources God had placed in local disciples. Nathan came to accept that he was not the key to fulfilling the Great Commission in north India. His ministry had to die. He had to become the kernel of wheat that falls to the ground. The vision to reach north India, Nepal and Bhutan was right. He was called by God, and he had to learn the most basic lesson for a movement pioneer. It wasn't about him but about God and his mission. It was about God and the resources he had placed in the lives of ordinary believers.

To become a movement pioneer, Nathan had to look beyond himself. He had to look past his efforts, his schedule and his achievements as the strategy. He was never going to be enough.

Nathan studied Jesus' ministry in the Gospel of Mark. He compared Jesus' public ministry to the crowds with his private

ministry to the disciples he called out from the crowds. Jesus'
private ministry was the key to changing the world—Jesus' time
with the disciples on the road, his sharing on their trips across
the lake, his taking them aside to explain things, his time alone
with them in the garden of Gethsemane. Nathan discovered
Jesus as a movement pioneer.

Jesus laid the foundation for a missionary movement by
training his disciples. Nathan was ready to do the same. He
began to see God's people as the key to fulfilling what God had
put on his heart. He realized that vision could be limited by
rules about "who can and who can't": Who can and who can't
evangelize? Who can and who can't baptize? Who can and who
can't make disciples? Who can and who can't plant a church?

Nathan realized that if his vision was to plant one church
every year, he could limit the ministry to paid professionals. But
if the vision was for one thousand churches in a year, he had to
mobilize every believer to do the ministry. They must be given
real responsibility and real authority.

A vision shaped by God's grace will demand urgency, faith
and taking risks. Nathan was compelled to release ordinary
people to spread the gospel, make disciples, plant and multiply churches.

Jeff Sundell challenged Nathan to offer training in multiplying disciples and churches to as many believers as possible.
He challenged Nathan to train at least five hundred people each
year. Jeff urged him to find the 8–10 percent of trainees who
would be faithful and fruitful, and to equip them to train others.
Then of those 8–10 percent Nathan was to identify five to spend
sixty to ninety days a year training and encouraging.

Nathan rewrote his job description. Then he began to train.

He put simple tools in the hands of ordinary disciples and sent them out. Nathan trained them in the five parts of a church-planting movement (CPM) plan:

1. How do we enter a new field and connect with lost people?

2. How do we share the gospel? What do we say?

3. When people say yes to following Jesus, how do we train disciples?

4. How do we gather disciples into new communities? How do we form churches?

5. How do we multiply workers?[2]

Nathan wanted every disciple to know how to do these things. As he trained, he identified the workers who were faithful and fruitful. One of them was Lipok.

FROM DRUG USER TO DISCIPLE MAKER

Lipok is from Nagaland, a state in far northeastern India. The Nagas have been staunchly Christian for 150 years. So when Lipok began using drugs, his parents thought the solution was to send him to Bible college. Instead, his drug and alcohol abuse increased, and he graduated in 1990 with a bachelor of theology degree and a heroin addiction.

He soon found himself in prison, where he met members of the resistance movement who were fighting India and Burma for an independent Nagaland. On his release he crossed the border into Burma and joined the cause, serving as a captain and as an assistant to the Naga prime minister in exile.

Opium is easy to come by in Burma; his drug habit grew worse. Finally he was arrested and imprisoned by the Indian authorities for his rebel activities. In prison he grew weary of his drug and alcohol addiction, and he became disillusioned with the rebel cause. He wanted to return to his faith but couldn't break free of his addictions.

After he was released he received news that his father had died. Lipok was still close to his father, who had never given up hope that his son would change. The news of his father's death came as a deep shock, which shook Lipok out of this dependence on drugs and alcohol. Lipok decided it was time to get right with God.

A theological education had not changed his heart. He needed to personally know God's love and forgiveness. In 2002 Lipok signed up for discipleship training with Youth With a Mission (YWAM). It was everything he had hoped for. God healed and forgave the lost years as a prodigal. After this time in YWAM, God called him to go back to Burma and share the gospel with his former rebel comrades, which he did, and some accepted Christ.

While he was living on the border, Lipok became aware of the Mising people of the Indian state of Assam scattered along the Brahmaputra River. God challenged him to tell them about Jesus.[3] The Mising people live along the fertile riverbeds of the Brahmaputra in thatched houses raised on stilts, which provide protection from floods and wild animals. When the floodwaters rise, the Mising pack up their few possessions and move across the river or downstream to other houses on stilts. The Mising face floods, malaria and waterborne diseases, yet they continue to live along the banks and tributaries of their beloved river because they regard it as holy.

Lipok began connecting and sharing the gospel with the

Mising, and he baptized the first Mising believer in August 2003. Other Mising people believed, and Lipok planted three new churches along the Brahmaputra.

The only church model Lipok knew was the one in Nagaland. To him, a church plant was complete when it had its own building. Soon Lipok discovered that he couldn't build churches fast enough to reach all of the Mising people. He wanted to see multiplication but didn't know how.

In July 2006 Lipok attended a training event on church-planting movements. Through the training Lipok grasped the importance of mobilizing new believers to reach their worlds and plant churches—just as Jesus sent the Samaritan woman into her town. He teamed up with Nathan Shank, and they began training disciples for multiplication. They trained, traveled and lived together.

Lipok already had a team of thirty frontline evangelists. Their task was to win people to Christ and bring them to one of the three existing churches. The strategy was reasonably successful. So Lipok was surprised when Nathan challenged his approach, pointing out that the evangelists were a bottleneck to multiplication. They were being paid to do what every believer should be trained to do.

"Then what should the thirty workers be doing?" Lipok wondered. Nathan helped him see that these evangelists could equip new disciples to spread the gospel and make disciples. Reading the New Testament convinced Lipok that every disciple has the authority to baptize and celebrate the Lord's Supper. He redefined his workers' roles from evangelists to church planters.

Lipok began training every disciple—most of whom were simple farmers—to share the gospel and make disciples. He empowered the disciples to plant churches among new believers. Immediately, new churches began springing up among the Mising, among Nepalis in the region, and among the Advashi and Chakma peoples. By the end of 2006 the three churches had become sixty churches.

Lipok and his workers planted churches up and down the Brahmaputra River system by training ordinary believers and releasing them with authority and responsibility. One local worker accounted for three hundred churches in his stream of multiplying churches.

In 2007 Jeff Sundell returned to visit the work in South Asia. He told Nathan that God had given him a vision of the Holy Spirit rolling down the Brahmaputra River. For some reason the number ten thousand was in his head. He told Nathan that as the Spirit moved down the Brahmaputra River, it would spill over into the rest of India.

By the end of 2014 Lipok believes they have reached the goal of ten thousand new churches.[4] He is now turning his attention to other unreached and unengaged people groups in north India and Nepal.

HOW THE SON OF A HINDU PRIEST MET JESUS

In 2007 Nathan began looking for opportunities to open up new streams of church planting. He approached some existing denominations to offer training and came under attack from leaders who saw this as a threat to their authority. Their denominations had not been involved in church planting for seventy-five years.

In the midst of a time of discouragement Nathan visited a sixty-year-old prayer warrior. He didn't share any of his concerns with her before she announced, "You are under great tension. You must endure! One month from now, it will only be a memory. God will do in six months what you thought was only possible in ten years!"

The next day, Nathan met Kumar. Kumar was from a Hindu high-caste family of temple builders in north India. But when Kumar was two years old, his father died and his three older brothers were sent to an orphanage because his mother could not afford to keep them. To support Kumar and his baby sister, she worked as a day laborer.

When he was eight years old, Kumar was desperate for an education and sought out a local Christian school where the principal gave him a scholarship on the condition that Kumar support himself working in the laundry and cooking.

As the eldest remaining son, Kumar was responsible to perform priestly duties at the Hindu temple. He spent every Friday in eight hours of prayer and meditation, after which he would bless those who came to the temple. But Kumar had no peace in his heart. His mind would often return to the question of how he could get to heaven.

One day while meditating he saw a vision in which he learned that the God of gods would come to him. Later he was shopping for idols when he saw a picture of Jesus on display. He bought the picture, took it home, and began to pray to and meditate on Jesus.

When he was fourteen, Kumar had another vision in which angels revealed heaven to him and told him of the coming day of judgment, which frightened him. He saw Jesus in the vision but felt he was not worthy to approach him. Kumar was torn between loyalty to his mother, his responsibility as the son of a Hindu priest and the growing desire to follow Jesus. His final break with Hinduism came when he was seventeen. He decided to be a disciple of Jesus and seek baptism. That same day his mother asked him to leave home and not return.

Now a high-school graduate, Kumar had to find a place to live and a way to provide for himself. He became a mathematics tutor to high school students. The money he earned was enough to live on and put himself through college.

Kumar's students did well, and demand for his tutoring grew. Soon, he was taking on more and more students. Kumar set up a boarding house for students living away from home. Eventually, he had ninety students under his care, all while he was studying full time at college.

During vacations, when the students returned to their homes, Kumar would go into the countryside of West Bengal and Sikkim to plant churches. When he had led enough people to Christ in an area, he would find a piece of land and build a church. He set a goal before God of one hundred new churches by 2020.

By 2007 Kumar had planted eleven new churches. Most people would be encouraged by such progress. Kumar, though, was devastated. His goal was one hundred new churches, and he had just thirteen years to plant another eighty-nine. At his current rate of progress he would not succeed. There just wasn't enough time in his schedule, and he couldn't afford to keep financing his trips to the countryside. For two months he prayed with bitter tears, asking God to either release him from his commitment or show him how he could do it. At the end of the two months of prayer, Kumar met Nathan Shank.

In July 2007 Nathan was in town to train people in church-planting movements. Kumar was too busy with his students to attend, but he did make it for one session. That one hour with Nathan changed his life. In sixty minutes Nathan summarized the training of the five parts of a CPM plan—entry, gospel, disciples, churches and multiplication. Kumar knew immediately what he needed to do.

Looking at the five parts, Kumar could see what he was doing well. He knew how to enter an unreached town and how to share the gospel. He even knew how to form new believers into a church and hand that church over to the denomination. Then he would move on to a new village and begin again. What he missed was training new believers in discipleship.

Kumar realized he was planting traditional churches in which new believers were passively dependent on him rather than actively making disciples themselves. Kumar saw that multiplication would not happen unless he discipled new believers to share the gospel, make disciples and form new churches. Now his goal of one hundred new churches was feasible.

Without delay, Kumar began training new believers to share the gospel with their neighbors. He told them, "Don't bring your friends and family to my house. Meet with them in your home. Even better, begin a new church in their home."

But Kumar had one more hurdle to overcome. The greatest obstacle was planted deeply in his own thinking. As Kumar began empowering new believers to make disciples and plant churches, Nathan explained the importance of releasing responsibility and authority to them. That meant giving disciples the authority to baptize and celebrate the Lord's Supper. Kumar drew the line. He was convinced that those tasks could only be performed by the clergy, not by ordinary disciples. Despite his radical edge, Kumar was locked into his church tradition.

Nathan took him through the Scriptures and showed him how the Great Commission gave authority to every believer to share the gospel, baptize and train disciples in obeying Jesus' commands. Kumar agreed his church tradition had to bow to Scripture.

One of Kumar's disciples was an illiterate street sweeper from a low-caste background who took the name Israel. From 4 to 9 each morning Israel swept the streets. Despite his background he was proud of his job and won many government awards for the quality of his work.

Kumar trained Israel to share his new faith. Israel couldn't read, so his twelve-year-old daughter helped him learn Bible stories by heart. Then he used them to share the gospel and train new disciples.

Israel decided he wanted to learn to read the Bible for himself, so he put aside his pride and went with his daughter to her afterschool tutoring in Hindi. He stood outside the classroom and listened to the lesson through the closed door. When the tutor wondered what he was doing, Israel told him he wanted to make sure his daughter was getting good instruction for the money he was paying. Eventually, the tutor invited Israel into the room, and he joined the class of twelve-year-olds.

Israel was already connecting with lost people, finding persons of peace, sharing the gospel and discipling new believers. That would normally be enough for a semiliterate, low-caste street sweeper. But not for Israel.

Kumar trained him to plant churches. He taught Israel how to baptize new disciples and form them into new churches. On one occasion Kumar accompanied Israel as he visited an unreached community. When Israel led someone to Christ, Kumar challenged him to baptize the new disciple. At first, Israel was reluctant, then he agreed. They walked around the neighborhood until they found a pond big enough, and Israel performed his first baptism while Kumar watched.

Later that day, Kumar and Israel visited Israel's elderly father. When Israel's father heard that his son, the street sweeper, had been trusted to baptize a new Christian, he wept. His son, from such a low caste, had been honored with real responsibility.

Israel wasn't the same. Neither was Kumar, who was now convinced that he must let go of his ministry and empower street sweepers and rickshaw drivers to do the ministry of Jesus.

On August 31, 2008, Kumar reached his goal of one hundred new churches, twelve years ahead of time. Immediately, he asked God what's next. The answer came, "Train the hundred churches to plant three churches each."

Kumar trained his local church leaders. They trained their people. Some churches planted five new churches. Others planted none. By the beginning of 2009 the network of 100 churches had grown to 422. What did Kumar do next? He trained the 422 churches to plant three more churches each. Today, like Lipok, Kumar's work continues to multiply. The vision for ten thousand churches has been surpassed.

There are over 600,000 villages in India alone. Of those villages, 420,000 have no evangelical presence. Nathan, Kumar and Lipok are using the keys to reaching them. One of those keys is leadership development at every level.

THAT'S WHY WE'RE HERE

For over a hundred years members of Nathan Shank's family have served Christ in north India and Nepal. None of them have seen a multiplying movement—until now.

Realistically, tens of thousands of new disciples and thousands of new churches are nothing compared to more than one
billion people of South Asia. Nathan knows that. He has no
illusions about the magnitude of the task. Nathan refuses to
shrink his vision to fit reality. He is adamant that it must be as
grand and as extravagant as the grace of God in Jesus Christ.
He says, "That's why we're here—to catalyze church-planting
movements across north India and the surrounding nations."

Nathan Shank, Lipok and Kumar are inspired by Paul's example of "no place left" throughout the eastern half of the
Roman Empire (Romans 15:23). For Paul, that meant he planted
churches in major centers that would continue to reach each
region in depth. Like Paul, they work toward a day when their
work of pioneering and multiplying churches throughout a vast
region will continue so they can move on to new fields. Like
Paul, these men want to be able to say one day, "There is no place
left for us in north India, Nepal and Bhutan." Nathan Shank,
Lipok and Kumar are movement pioneers.

PIONEER PROFILE

William Taylor, Troublemaker and Bishop

No one in the second half of the nineteenth century comes close to the contribution of William Taylor in extending the boundaries of the Methodist movement beyond Europe and North America.[1]

His father, Stuart Taylor, was converted at a Methodist camp meeting in the hills of Virginia in 1832 and soon became an evangelist. William was converted nine years later at another camp meeting. Before the camp meeting broke up William was preaching in the streets. A year later, when he was twenty-one, his father provided William with a horse, saddle, bridle and saddlebags filled with clothing and books. William Taylor set off as a newly appointed "junior preacher." Seven years later he went out as a Methodist missionary to the California gold fields, sailing from Baltimore to San Francisco with his wife and young child. He was now twenty-eight.

William Taylor made things happen. In San Francisco he built a home for his family with his own hands. He preached in bars and on the streets of California's fast-growing towns. He nursed the sick, aided the poor, defended Native Americans and ministered in the Chinese labor camps and among the sailors in the port area. When ministry funds ran out, Taylor had to return to the east to raise money through speaking and the sale of his book, *Seven Years Street Preaching in San Francisco*.

Among the thousands lured to California looking for gold, hundreds found faith in Christ through William Taylor and were gathered into self-supporting churches.

It was now time to take the lessons learned on the US frontier to the wider world. In 1849 Taylor left California and for the next nine years toured New England, the Midwest, Canada, Australia and New Zealand on evangelistic missions.

He spent 1866–1868 in South Africa. White South Africans were unimpressed by his revivalist style and message, so he went to the black tribes and became an effective evangelist among the indigenous population. Taylor credited the remarkable impact of his preaching to the partnership he formed with his African translator, Charles Panda.

South Africa shaped Taylor's missionary methods. He rejected the mission-station model, in which missionaries became civil magistrates, preachers, school superintendents and supervisors of dependent African converts. He believed that formal training had made Africans ineffective preachers.[2] Instead, Taylor gave the most gifted African preachers basic training and sent them into the main population centers. He expected them to plant self-supporting churches and quickly move on to the next opportunity. Taylor's unprecedented success in South Africa led to invitations to minister in England, the Caribbean and eventually India.

Taylor arrived in India in 1870, penniless, as usual. There was no success among the Indians in the shadow of the mission compounds. At loose ends and still impoverished after months of fruitless efforts, Taylor struck out on his own. He preached in the large cities of southern India and planted churches in the former Bombay, Calcutta and dozens of other centers. He established self-supporting churches—equal, he argued, to any church in North America. Soon after a congregation was established, Taylor appointed a pastor and moved on to another city.

The Methodist Episcopal Mission Board was furious. Taylor did not have their permission for this expansion. And the work had been carried out in fields that were the responsibility of other denominations. Furthermore, the new churches under Taylor's influence would not accept financial support.

The Mission Board initiated a ten-year campaign to discredit the idea of self-supporting missions and to force the churches of South India to accept American money and control. It cut off the supply of new workers to Taylor, so he recruited his own volunteers. He raised the money and sent the workers himself, including the first Methodist Episcopal missionaries to Burma.

In response to his board's accusations he wrote a paper on his missionary methods. He reflected on his years in India and described the failures of the traditional approach to mission. He described how he went about establishing self-supporting churches in each city. Taylor argued that the goal of Paul's mission was independent churches who were self-supporting, entrusted with their own governance and committed to an evangelistic style that enabled them to grow according to their own cultural patterns.

Taylor pointed out that since the days of Wesley and Asbury this was how Methodism had always expanded. The pioneering work was done by a few zealous men and women and local preachers. As people were converted, a self-supporting church was established. He rejected the current approach in which a mission was sustained by great institutions with reputations to protect. This led to the missionaries becoming masters rather than servants.

Leaving India in 1877 Taylor arrived in South America. He was wary of the Mission Board's practice of providing too much financial support, which undermined the new converts' responsibility and resulted in dependency. He refused to place the mission under the board's control. So Taylor raised the funds and recruited the missionaries himself.[3]

The conflict with the Mission Board intensified. Taylor's missionaries for South America were drawn from holiness-revivalist groups on the fringes of Methodism. They were less educated and less cultured than the typical denominational missionary, but neither were they too proud to call the uneducated and uncultured Chileans their brothers. As one Presbyterian missionary observed, "There is a great deal of froth and bombast and other defects it is easy to point out, but the fact remains, the poor have the Gospel preached to them."[4] By 1906 that "froth and bombast" had produced a movement of four thousand believers in Chile.

Within the Methodist Episcopal Church, Taylor was admired for his energy and achievements, but distrusted for his independent spirit. In part to "promote" Taylor out of South America, he was elected as missionary bishop for Africa in 1884.

In Liberia Taylor discovered that the existing Methodist Episcopal churches, made up of freed North American slaves, were hopelessly addicted to subsidies. So he began planting self-supporting missions in the interior and along the south coast among indigenous tribes. He did the same in Angola, Congo and Mozambique.[5]

Despite his achievements in the field, in the twelve years of his appointment as missionary bishop he made no progress in changing the structures of the denomination and Mission Board that inhibited Methodist expansion.

Throughout his amazing career Taylor served in six continents. He was instrumental in establishing Methodist churches in Peru, Chile, South India, Burma, Panama, Belize, Brazil, Angola, Mozambique and Zaire. He partnered with the Wesleyan Methodist movement to plant churches in Australia, New Zealand, Ceylon (Sri Lanka), South Africa and throughout the Caribbean.

In the second half of the nineteenth century William Taylor was the primary driver of the global expansion of Methodism. Sadly, movement pioneers like William Taylor increasingly became the exception within Methodism. Yet his example and mission strategy had a profound influence on the Keswick tradition of holiness missions and on the global spread of Pentecostalism in the twentieth century.

six

Five Levels of
Movement Leadership

> *Every believer a church planter, every*
> *church a church-planting church.*
>
> Alan Hirsch and Dave Ferguson,
> *On the Verge*

We have seen how movement pioneers take the gospel into unreached territory. They train new disciples to obey what Jesus commanded, to form new churches and to reach their communities. Like Paul, they have a "no place left" end vision. This is only possible with a strategy that produces multiple streams of reproducing churches.

The key to achieving "no place left" is the development of leadership at every level of a movement. By *leadership* I don't mean someone who occupies a position but someone who makes things happen.

We can identify five levels of leadership in a multiplying movement of disciples and churches—seed sowers, church planters, church multipliers, multiplication trainers and movement catalysts.[1]

LEVEL 1: SEED SOWER

A *seed sower* is a disciple who obeys Jesus' command to spread the gospel (see fig. 6.1). Every believer should be a seed sower.

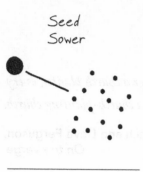

Seed Sower

Figure 6.1.

Seed sowers master simple tools such as knowing a gospel presentation, sharing their personal testimonies of God's work in their lives and leading a Discovery Bible Study. They know what to say and with whom to share. Sowers are motivated by God's love for lost people. They reach out to their families and friends, or they find ways to enter unreached fields looking for people of peace.

To mobilize seed sowers, Nathan trained five hundred people in 2006 to share the gospel. He challenged trainees to share their stories or the gospel story with five people every week. He identified forty-seven sowers who won at least one entire family to Christ that year. Nathan equipped them to train others. Ten of those forty-seven began training others. Nathan challenged each of the ten to train five hundred people.

By 2009 Nathan and his trainees were training five thousand people a year to share the gospel. That year ten thousand people a month were hearing the gospel, and an average of forty-six new believers were baptized each day.

As God begins to work through new believers, their motivation becomes intrinsic. The Holy Spirit meets them in the task and confirms their partnership. The new believers discover God the Holy Spirit working through them to spread the gospel and make disciples.

The strategy of training every believer to share the gospel, share their stories and facilitate Discovery Bible Studies is proving to be effective throughout the world.

The next challenge for a seed sower is to learn how to train new disciples and form them into churches.

LEVEL 2: CHURCH PLANTER

Church planters are seed sowers who have learned how to make disciples and plant churches (see fig. 6.2). Using simple Discovery Bible Study methods, they teach new disciples how to begin following and obeying what Jesus commanded. They equip new believers to become seed sowers.

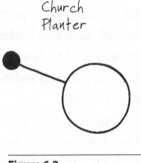

Church planters accept their authority to baptize new believers and teach them how to celebrate the Lord's Supper. Using simple methods, they train disciples to obey

Figure 6.2.

what they learn. They form disciples into groups that become churches, based on the characteristics of the church in Acts 2.

Steve Smith has four suggestions for church planters who want to help discipleship groups become churches.

1. Know what you are trying to achieve: a clear definition of when a group becomes a church.

2. When you start a training group, model the parts of church life from the very beginning.

3. Make sure you have a specific lesson or lessons on church and its ordinances in your early discipleship.

4. Use church health mapping (see below) to help a group evaluate if they have all the elements of church life.[2]

Effective church planters release authority and responsibility to local leaders (1 Timothy 3:1-7; Titus 1:5-9; 1 Peter 5:1-4).[3] Does Paul allow new believers to be appointed as leaders? Not in Ephesus; he tells Timothy that a leader should not be a new believer. However, in Paul's instructions to Titus, on Crete, he removes that requirement. Why the difference? Ephesus was an established church. Crete was a newly planted church.[4] Luke tells us that Paul appointed elders in newly established churches (Acts 14:23). With prayer and fasting, Paul and Barnabas committed these new leaders to the Lord. As a church planter Paul worked hard to develop local leaders, but he also knew when to commit a church and its leaders to the Lord while he moved on to new fields.

Typically, in church-planting movements seed sowers and church planters are not paid salaries, although the cost of their training is often covered.

The next challenge for a church planter is to learn how to multiply churches, not just add them.

Helping groups become churches. To see church multiplication it's important to identify how discipleship groups form into churches. Following is a simple health diagnostic for new discipleship groups and churches. Leaders assess each health characteristic and identify weaknesses and action plans.[5]

In figure 6.3, a solid line indicates a group has completed studies. A broken line indicates a group that is meeting for Discovery Bible Study but is not yet functioning or identifying itself as a church. Symbols are inside the circle if the functions they represent are practiced by local believers, and outside the circle if they are not being practiced or if they are performed by someone outside of the local community.

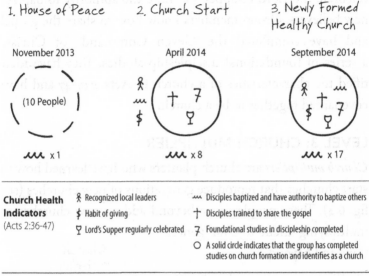

Figure 6.3. Helping groups become churches

1. *House of peace.* The first group is a Discovery Bible Study that has been meeting in the home of a new believer since November 2013. Ten people attend, and one of them has been baptized.

2. *Church start.* The second group has become a new church start. There are eight baptized believers. They have completed seven studies in foundational discipleship. Members can share the gospel with others. They celebrate the Lord's Supper and give regularly. The dollar sign is outside the circle because the group is not yet responsible to decide what is done with the money collected. Local leadership has not yet been identified and new disciples are relying on an outside leader for baptisms.

3. *Newly formed healthy church.* The third group on the right is a newly formed church. There are seventeen baptized believers and an identified local leader. The members give regularly. They celebrate the Lord's Supper and have the authority to baptize new believers. Group members know how to share the gospel and have completed the "Seven Commands of Christ," a series of foundational discipleship studies. They have identified the characteristics of a church in Acts 2:36-47 and have covenanted together to be a church.

LEVEL 3: CHURCH MULTIPLIER

Church multipliers are church planters who have learned how to start churches that reproduce generations of new churches (see fig. 6.4). These people move beyond adding new churches to multiplying them to four generations and beyond.

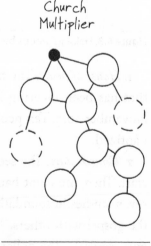

1. *First-generation churches* are started by the original church planter. They represent growth by addition.

2. *Second-generation churches* are started by disciples from first-generation churches who were trained by the original church planter. They represent the beginning of growth by multiplication.

Figure 6.4.

3. *Third-generation churches and beyond* follow the same pattern as second-generation churches. Each new generation is en-

couraged to take responsibility to target its own fields. When fourth-generation churches become the norm, a church-planting movement has emerged.

Church multipliers identify and equip seed sowers and church planters. They release authority and responsibility to the leaders they are developing. They understand the characteristics of healthy churches, and diagnose and handle the health of a network of churches. They test and strengthen correct doctrine and correct behavior among the churches.

Church multipliers do not pastor and grow one church; they want to see multiple generations of churches. Following Paul's example (Acts 20:17-38), they release authority to local leaders and their churches. Committing them to the Holy Spirit and the living Word of God, church multipliers then seek out unreached fields.

Church multipliers are critical to the emergence and growth of a movement. They represent the leadership transition from addition to multiplication. This is the most important and the most difficult transition of all. The lack of level 3 leaders is a major reason for the lack of church-planting movements in the Western world, where church planting is typically by addition, not multiplication.

A church multiplier's next challenge is to equip other multipliers to achieve third- and fourth-generation churches.

LEVEL 4: MULTIPLICATION TRAINER

Multiplication trainers are church multipliers who have learned how to equip other church multipliers to achieve third- and fourth-generation churches (see fig. 6.5).

The key difference between level 3 and level 4 leaders is that level 4 leaders influence and train beyond their own networks or streams of reproducing churches.

In a church-planting movement, multiplication trainers preferably have field experience in getting from "zero to church."[6]

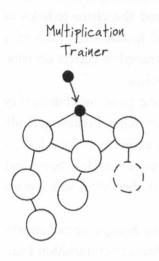

Multiplication Trainer

They can enter an unreached community, reach lost people and help the new disciples form a new church. They also train others to move from zero to church. They win the trust of leaders of other networks of churches and help them progress to fourth-generation churches. By training and releasing others, they minister beyond the limitations of their own abilities.

Figure 6.5.

Multiplication trainers learn from effective practitioners in different fields. They identify and remove barriers to multiplication across different streams of church planting and manage the complexities of multiple streams of church planting. As advocates for church-planting movements, they help others grasp the paradigm of multiplying movements. They win over skeptics by responding to objections and criticisms. They train and mobilize networks beyond their own networks of multiplying churches. Effective multiplication trainers help others get to third- and fourth-generation churches.

There is one final leadership level: *movement catalyst*. For multiplication trainers to become movement catalysts, they need a

Revelation 7 vision to reach every nation, tribe, people and language: "After this I looked, and there before me was a great multitude that no one could count, from every nation, tribe, people and language, standing before the throne and before the Lamb" (Revelation 7:9).

LEVEL 5: MOVEMENT CATALYST

The key difference between a multiplication trainer (level 4) and a level 5 leader is that a *movement catalyst* takes on a broad responsibility to reach an unreached population segment or region (see fig. 6.6).

Movement Catalyst

These leaders are the catalysts for multiple streams of church planting within a previously unengaged and unreached people group. They are advocates for a vision to finish the task among a people group, a local area, a nation or a region of the world. They train leaders on levels 1-4. They mobilize resources and oversee the implementation of a multiplying church-planting strategy. (To understand how all five levels relate, see figure 6.7.)

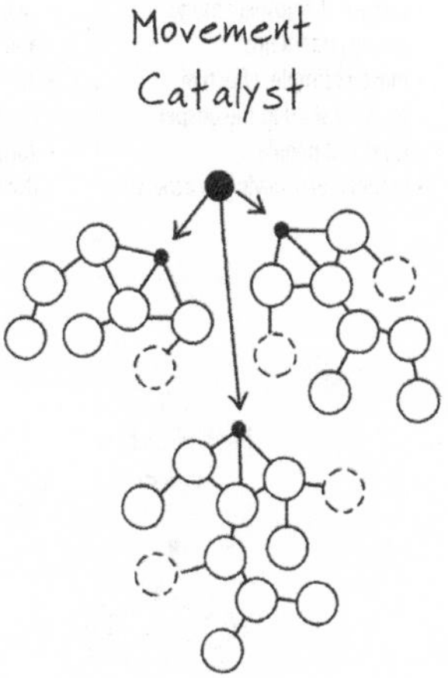

Figure 6.6.

The apostle Paul fulfilled this role as a movement pioneer who started multiple streams of church planting from Jerusalem to Illyricum (Romans 15:19).[7] Nathan Shank functions as a movement catalyst in South Asia. He has accepted the responsibility to reach a field of 480 million people. He began by sharing

L1 Seed Sower	L2 Church Planter	L3 Church Multiplier
A disciple who • spreads the gospel among family and friends • masters simple, effective tools for sharing the gospel • loves lost people • models seed sowing to others	A level 1 leader who • learns how to make disciples and plant churches • trains level 1 workers to share the gospel • forms disciples into groups that become churches	A level 2 leader who • starts churches that reproduce churches to four generations • equips level 1 and level 2 leaders • ensures the health of churches and releases authority to local leaders

L4 Multiplication Trainer	L5 Movement Catalyst
A level 3 leader who • produces four generations of new churches across multiple streams of church planting • engages beyond the leader's own network to cast vision and train for multiplication • identifies and resolves barriers to multiplication	A level 4 leader who • becomes a catalyst for multiple streams of church planting among unreached people groups • equips level 3 and level 4 leaders to facilitate multiple streams of multiple generations of church planting • majors in networking, resourcing and vision casting

Figure 6.7. Five levels of leadership

the gospel and planting churches. He partnered with local leaders to train hundreds of seed sowers; some became church planters. He helped church planters become church multipliers. He identified local leaders and equipped them to become multiplication trainers. He is now working to help Lipok and Kumar step into the role of movement catalyst (see chap. 5).

Jeff Sundell is an example of a movement catalyst in a Western setting. He has trained broadly throughout the United States and built a network of church multipliers and multiplication trainers. He is casting a vision for reaching fifty US cities where a majority of the people are ethnic minorities. He trains and mobilizes leaders from levels 1-4. He coaches level 3 and level 4 leaders, and builds networks between them.

GROWING LEVEL 1 TO LEVEL 5 LEADERS

Movements expect every believer to share the gospel and make disciples. These are spiritual disciplines for every follower of Jesus. Perhaps 10 percent of seed sowers become church planters. The percentages get even smaller as we move to level 3, level 4 and level 5 leaders.

There is no automatic progression from level 1 to level 5. Some church planters should remain effective church planters. They may make poor church multipliers. Some very effective level 3 to level 5 leaders were not as effective as sowers and planters. Leaders need to find their personal levels of giftedness and calling. There is not a hierarchy of value between the levels of leadership. As we will see, a leader can only progress to the next level by becoming a servant who empowers others.

The critical transition is helping church planters become

church multipliers. This transition marks the boundary between addition and multiplication. Most church planting in the West focuses on starting and growing the next church. Movements focus on multiple generations of churches.

When Nathan Shank met Lipok and Kumar, they were both functioning as church planters (L2). He helped them through the transition from church planter to church multiplier (L3) by teaching them to release authority. Lipok and Kumar had to encourage their seed sowers (L1) to become church planters (L2). As these two men took on a training role, they helped church planters (L2) become church multipliers (L3) who led streams of church planting that resulted in multiple generations of new churches.

What did that look like? A major barrier to multiplication was Lipok's and Kumar's church traditions. They were reluctant to release authority and responsibility to ordinary believers. They believed that only ordained clergy could baptize believers, perform the Lord's Supper and plant churches.

Kumar empowered Israel, the street sweeper, to move from sower (L1) to church planter (L2). In doing so, Kumar moved from church planter to church multiplier (L3). In this paradigm disciples step up to a new level of leadership by helping those around them do the same.

Jeff Sundell challenged Nathan Shank to spend sixty to ninety days of each year with leaders, like Lipok and Kumar, who are multiplying. Lipok and Kumar have learned from Nathan to do the same.

Figure 6.8 shows how an effective level 5 leader will make it a priority to help church planters become church multipliers, and church multipliers become multiplication trainers.

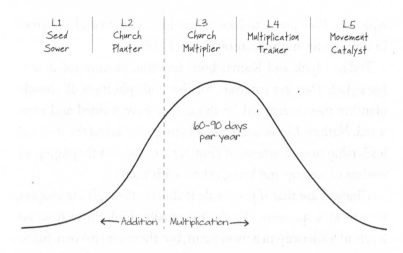

Figure 6.8. Moving from addition to multiplication. Movement catalysts should spend 60 to 90 days per year over 2 to 3 years equipping and mentoring L3 and L4 leaders. The dotted line represents the transition from addition to multiplication.

The bell curve shows that a movement catalyst spends less time equipping sowers and other movement catalysts, located at either end of the graph. The church planter's job is to train, mobilize and coach sowers. At the other end of the scale, movement catalysts (once they are established) need less input. The critical transition is from church planter to church multiplier. Jeff and Nathan have learned to put time and energy into helping leaders cross over from ministry by addition to ministry by multiplication.

INVESTING TIME AND ENERGY IN MULTIPLYING LEADERS

Most churches and mission agencies invest their time and resources in leaders who share the gospel and plant churches (L1 and L2). That's addition. In contrast, movement pioneers believe sharing the gospel and planting churches is what ordinary disciples do. They prefer to invest their limited time and resources in training for multiplication (L3 to L5).[8]

Today, Lipok and Kumar both function as movement catalysts (L5). They are catalysts for the multiplication of church-planting movements led by those they have trained and mentored. Nathan, Lipok and Kumar continually assess the levels of leadership in each stream of church planting, and they equip all leaders to step up and bring others with them.

Chances are that if you made it this far through the chapter, your head is spinning. We don't normally think this way about levels of leadership in a movement, but there are two benefits to viewing leadership in this manner. First, understanding levels of leadership helps stretch our vision. It enables us to think beyond planting the next church to beginning a church-planting movement. Second, everyone can find his or her place in these levels, from seed sower to movement catalyst, and ask what's next. How do we take the next step in our development and bring others with us? We all have our roles to play. We can all improve on our current leadership level and grow into the next.

Perhaps you haven't begun to share your faith with others. You can learn to become a seed sower. Maybe you can lead others to Christ, but you need to focus on making disciples and forming churches. And you need to train those disciples to share their faith. You can become a church planter. Or perhaps you've planted churches but never considered the possibility of multiplying churches. Once you're training others to plant churches that multiply, you need to trust God for movements that reach cities, nations and people groups.

PIONEER PROFILE

Victor Landero, Columbian Apostle

Pedro Gutierrez sat behind the locked door of his small room waiting for dawn. It was 1949 and Columbia was in the grip of a civil war known as La Violencia. Pedro was a pastor-evangelist who once again had left the relative safety of the city behind to take the gospel to villages. He was in Providencia, a rural town that was known as a refuge for men who lived beyond the law.[1] He came to preach in the town square and sell Bibles.

It was 2 a.m. when he was startled by a pounding on his door and a voice shouting, "Are you the man who was selling Bibles? I want one!" It was Victor Landero, who ran both a bar and a brothel, and lived with three women. Someone had told Victor the Bible would explain how God made the world. He paid for the Bible and left.

Victor was illiterate, so he locked the Bible away in a box where it stayed for the next eight years. Eventually, Victor taught himself to read and began reading the Bible for the first time.

Soon after he had begun reading the Bible a young man named Eliezer Benavidez walked up to Victor as he sat reading on his front porch. Eliezer spoke to him about Jesus and showed him from the Bible how he could be saved. Over the next few weeks Eliezer kept returning until Victor finally surrendered to Christ as his Savior and Lord. Victor turned his cantina into a general store, closed his brothel and sent away two of his mistresses. The third stayed after putting her faith in Christ. They eventually married.

In 1958 the civil war ended and it was safe for missionaries to return to the Columbian interior. David Howard, the new field director of Latin American Missions, sent Robert Reed to investigate reports of new groups of believers springing up in the remote regions of Cordoba. Reed traveled by bus, jeep, canoe and on foot to Corozalito. Everywhere he went he met new groups of believers. The story was the same: Victor Landero had brought the gospel to them and gathered them into churches meeting in homes. Around one thousand believers gathered in over twenty groups in what was supposed to be an unevangelized region.

Eventually Howard met Victor Landero and learned how Victor had won his mother, father and ten brothers and sisters to Christ. Then he traveled from his village along the rivers and trails sharing the gospel with everyone he met. Once he'd reached the region around his village, he sold his farm and moved to an unreached area along the San Pedro River.

By 1963 there were two to three thousand disciples meeting in new churches. Still Victor could not settle down. One night in a dream God showed him a house in the jungle. Inside he was preaching to a group of people. Landero set out to look for the house and found it after two days. A woman answered the door, and Victor asked if he could hold an evangelistic meeting in her home that night. She agreed. Thirty-four people that night accepted Christ. Victor stayed a few days and formed the new believers into a new church.

Victor Landero was a movement pioneer. He would not settle down to pastor one church but was constantly on the move. Most of the converts were poor, uneducated farmers. He took new disciples with him on mission trips to learn from his example. When they were ready, he sent them out two-by-two to preach the gospel and plant churches. They appointed local leaders and returned regularly to strengthen and encourage the disciples.

Life in the churches was characterized by obedience to the Word, local leadership, openness to the power of the Holy Spirit and intense prayer. Victor did not identify himself or his churches as Pentecostal, yet their experience of the Holy Spirit included speaking in tongues, casting out demons and healing the sick. The churches were organized into circuits. New believers were immediately involved in evangelism and church planting. Leaders were trained on the job. The movement did not seek outside leadership or financial support.

In 1965 David Howard asked a meeting of about one hundred adults how many had been led to Christ by a missionary or pastor. Not one hand was raised. When he asked how many had been led to Christ by a neighbor, every hand went up.

Victor Landero is just one example of the twentieth-century shift in Christianity's center of gravity. That shift has been away from Europe and the European-derived cultures to Africa, Asia and Latin America. The regions of the world with the fastest growing Christian communities are those with the fastest growing populations.[2]

Movement pioneers like Victor Landero have led the way. And the people of Africa, Asia and Latin America have provided their time, energy and resources to make it happen.

seven

No Place Left in America

> *St. Paul did not go about as a missionary preacher merely*
> *to convert individuals: he went to establish Churches*
> *from which the light might radiate throughout*
> *the whole country around.*

Roland Allen, *Missionary Methods:*
St. Paul's or Ours?

It was November 2012. I was in Chesnee, South Carolina, tagging along with movement pioneer Jeff Sundell to learn how he trained workers for disciple-making movements.[1] Lunch was to be with three of his guys—Neil, Dean and Clint—who showed up forty-five minutes late. They had been raking leaves. Every Thursday, these three men visited this semirural community looking for persons of peace—people in whom God was already at work. Their aim was to get into homes to do Discovery Bible Studies.

Chesnee has it tough economically. Over the last twenty years all the textile mills have shut down. There are no jobs, and people are moving out in search of work. People are also moving in because houses are cheap. But there are no jobs.

As the guys walked the neighborhoods, they prayed for divine appointments. That morning they met Johnny, who was sitting on his porch as they walked by, and a conversation began. They asked the miracle question—"If God could do a miracle in your life, what would it be?"

Before long they were on the porch with Johnny, praying for healing for his painful back. They continued to chat and also met his dogs. Half an hour later, Johnny agreed to host a neighborhood Bible study in his home the next week. They met a few of Johnny's neighbors in the street and prayed for some more needs.

Then Neil, Dean and Clint met Suzanne. She was raking the leaves in her front yard. The brace and cast on her leg were a conversation starter. One of the three men asked her the miracle question. They prayed for her leg and soon discovered she had arrived in the community just the day before. She was on the run from a violent husband who had beaten her and injured her leg.

Suzanne was very grateful that there were people praying for her new community. She told them she thought God hated her because she had done so much wrong. One of the guys briefly shared his story of coming to faith in Christ and the gospel story. Then they invited her to the Discovery Bible Study beginning the next week across the road at Johnny's house.

By then, it was time for them to meet us for lunch. Instead, they took the rake from Suzanne, borrowed two more from Johnny's house and began raking the leaves. I suppose that was more important than arriving on time for a meeting with me!

That's not where the story ends. When Neil, Dean and Clint finally arrived at the restaurant, they greeted the waitress like a long-lost friend. They visited Chesnee every Thursday and in-tentionally ate at the same restaurant, wanting to get to know the staff. They knew Sally, the waitress, and the name of her partner, and they had already been praying for Sally's young son, who had been sick.

When Sally brought the meals, Dean asked, "How can we pray for you?" She answered, "Well, guys, I have a deadline to meet. We have to move out of our house by 1 p.m. on Friday, and I'm working. Everything has to be packed. The utilities have to be disconnected, and that moving van filled. I have to work tomorrow and my partner will have to do everything while he's looking after our son." So Dean prayed for Sally. Ten minutes later Sally came back, and the guys offered to help her partner pack the van the next day. Phone numbers were swapped.

Five houses visited. Four people prayed for. Two heard some-thing of the gospel. A neighborhood Bible study was launched, and an offer was made to help Sally and her family move to a new house in the area. Not bad for a morning's work.

BACK IN THE USA

Jeff Sundell spent ten years pioneering movements among Tibetan Buddhists in northern India and Nepal.[2] Jeff and his coworkers trained and equipped thousands of local believers to share the gospel and plant churches. Across the region tens of thousands of new disciples formed new, simple churches—many of them in places where there is official hostility toward Christianity.

In 2009 the Sundells moved back to the United States, where they began attending a local church. It took Jeff about three weeks of sitting in a church pew on Sundays before he said to himself, *I can't do this anymore!* So, Jeff began doing what he had done in South Asia. He went into the community looking for people who were far from God, getting into homes and leading people to Christ. He trained new disciples and formed new churches.

Word began to spread about what Jeff was doing, and it wasn't long before others, like Neil, Dean and Clint, joined him. He set the example and trained anyone who was willing to learn. The result is an expanding US network of practitioners and trainers.[3]

In 2012 I drove to a cabin in the Great Smoky Mountains to participate in a "Community of Practice" for people who were implementing the training. It was a chance to report in, identify progress and challenges, and plan next steps. We had all read the book of Acts. Jeff asked us to come prepared to identify lessons on the Holy Spirit, the spread of the gospel, the power of God in healing and miracles, the impact of persecution and the response to it, new disciples and new churches. As we identified lessons, they were written on large sheets of butcher paper hanging on the walls. Jeff wanted us to see that the world of Acts was also the world we serve.

Next, in small groups each practitioner answered these four questions:

1. What is God doing?
2. Where are you stuck (sharing the gospel, training disciples, forming churches)?
3. What two action plans would move you toward generational growth?
4. How can we pray for you?

Each person had about forty-five minutes to share the answers, to commit to new goals and to receive prayer. At the end of two days, each of us was commissioned to go back into the harvest.

I'M TOO OLD TO PLAY CHURCH!

Gary Stump was a successful businessman. He had been married for fourteen years when a drunk driver killed his wife, Donna, and left him with serious injuries and four children to raise.[4] In the grief and turmoil that followed the accident, all Gary could do was trust God for what he couldn't understand.

Out of tragedy Gary heard the call to leave the business world and become a pastor. In 1989 he entered seminary, and a year later he became the pastor of a struggling Baptist church with four members. Gary had married again in 1989. When he and Kathy, together with his four children, joined the church, their family increased the church rolls by 150 percent.

God breathed new life into that small church, and it grew to 220 people in worship, with most of them previously unchurched. Nine years later the church was running well. It had people, finances and leaders. Then God called Gary to a new assignment.

In 2000 Gary planted a church in Fishers, a town near Indianapolis. The church grew rapidly and soon needed larger facilities. By 2001 the church rented a facility to cope with the growing numbers. The monthly rent was $11,000. There was a worship band and large screens for multimedia. Then, in 2006, Gary merged his church plant with another church plant led by a close friend. By 2011 they had fifteen hundred people in worship and had planted two new churches. Between 2001 and 2011 the church baptized one thousand people. There were dozens of staff, capital campaigns and building programs. Total cost: $20 million. Yet after twenty years of ministry, and despite the outward success, Gary was questioning whether he was making disciples or just gathering a crowd.

Then someone gave him a copy of *T4T: Discipleship Re-Revolution* by Steve Smith and Ying Kai. This is the story of a disciple-making movement in East Asia, sparked by Ying Kai. Gary recounts how he read the first chapter and it "wrecked" him.

During the period when Gary's church had baptized a thousand people, Ying Kai launched a multiplying movement that planted 158,000 churches and baptized 1.7 million new believers. Gary realized his ministry was not enough to reach a lost world. Only a multiplying movement like Ying Kai experienced could do that. Gary concluded he was too old to play church any longer. He had to give up his obsession with the "ABCs"—attendance, buildings and cash.

Gary made an important shift. He no longer focused on Sunday morning programming as the center of church life. He said, "This leads to complicated, over-rehearsed programs that require an enormous drain on resources—both human and financial. It just seemed too complicated to me. We felt that the Lord was asking us to keep it simple."[5] Gary wanted to make disciples in such numbers that it would transform his community. He wanted to make an impact on families, schools and neighborhoods. He wanted to see lives changed by the gospel.

Gary left his church and began again. He planted Onward Church with the intention of multiplying disciples who make disciples. Gary didn't want to see just another church but a movement. He wasn't interested any longer in how many people turned up on a Sunday morning—although they do have Sunday morning services. Gary became concerned for one thing. He wanted to know, "Are we effective in bringing people to Christ, in making disciples and getting new disciples to immediately make disciples of others?"

Gary realized that in his two decades as a pastor he had encouraged, challenged, rebuked, motivated, inspired and even scolded Christians toward disciple making. But he had never taught anyone how to make a disciple.

Early in 2012 Gary opened up his basement and began training interested people in T4T (Training for Trainers), a method of making disciples and multiplying churches developed by Ying Kai.[6] He divided the church into eight groups of twenty-five people who met every other week. By the middle of the year he had trained two hundred people in how to make disciples.[7] Each lesson finished with fresh commitments to follow Jesus and to fish for people—with something to obey and someone to tell. Gary first trained a group of high school students. They led the way. He soon had twelve-year-old kids sharing their stories, sharing the gospel and starting Discovery Bible Studies.

Gary taught four different methods of inductive Bible study. All the Bible studies were participative, used self-discovery and were obedience oriented. The participants started by asking, "How have we obeyed what we learned last time?" Then they asked, "How have we been fishing?"

In January 2013 Gary launched a new series of eight Discovery Bible Studies, which provided an overview of the Bible from Genesis to Revelation. Many of the trainees discovered they had friends and family who were willing to study an overview of the Bible if only someone would invite them.

Gary was determined to train and mobilize everyone in the

life of the church. Jerry was one of those people. He reluctantly attended every training session. He told Gary, "Pastor, I'm only here because you invited me. Don't ever expect me to share my faith! I'm too shy. I'm too withdrawn. I'm too afraid. It's not gonna happen." But Jerry later led his grandson to Christ, took him through foundational discipleship and baptized him.

Jerry was one of many who got involved. By the end of 2013 there were two hundred groups with one thousand participants meeting in the community. Half of them were not followers of Christ when they joined a group.

When a group starts a second group, Gary identifies them as a second generation, and then a third generation and so forth. By 2014 Gary was seeing fifth- and sixth-generation groups form. That's multiplication.

When someone comes to Christ, the person who led them to Christ is equipped to disciple them. Immediately, new believers are encouraged and trained to share the gospel with their families and friends, to disciple others and to form groups.

Trainees learn how to share their stories, share God's story and to facilitate Discovery Bible Studies. Gary's trainees learn that any disciple can lead someone to Christ, baptize them and teach them to follow Jesus and fish for people. They baptize new disciples in swimming pools, bathtubs, hot tubs and lakes. The trainees learn that any disciple can form a new group around God's Word and fulfill the healthy functions of a church described in Acts 2:36-47.

Gary and his coworkers track each new generation of groups. It's hard keeping up with all the groups, especially when they reproduce beyond the fourth generation! (A large amount of good ministry is happening without Gary's knowledge.)

Ron is one of Gary's most effective workers. He had been in the same small group for ten years before he went through Gary's version of the T4T training. He launched a new Discovery Bible Study and then launched three more Discovery groups out of the original Discovery group. He left the first group to begin a group with lost people. In his opinion people have never really studied the Bible until they've studied it with someone who was far from God and is discovering the gospel for the first time. Ron continues to train groups and launch new ones. He has helped sixteen groups start and has one sixth-generation group.

Many of the groups remain part of the Onward Church. Some groups formed new churches but still relate to Onward. Gary is a both-and leader. He doesn't mandate whether a group should stay with Onward or form a new church, but he expects that they will all function as healthy expressions of the body of Christ. Onward still runs public worship on Sunday mornings. Gary is not opposed to larger gatherings but is more concerned that the gospel gets out through God's people, and that those people are equipped and released to make disciples and form new groups and churches as the need arises. He's working out the details as the story unfolds.

There has been a price to pay. As Gary and his church have engaged in the harvest, they have walked into a firestorm of spiritual warfare. In twenty-four years as a pastor, Gary has never seen so many bizarre and life-threatening illnesses in a church community. He takes this seriously as a spiritual battle they must face as they rescue people from the kingdom of darkness. He is not deterred.

Gary says the greatest challenge is developing workers to

keep pace with the multiplication of groups. He wants leaders who are godly and biblically sound.

Fishers, Indiana, is Gary Stump's Ephesus. When the apostle Paul was based in Ephesus, his ministry touched a city of 200,000 people. Meanwhile, Paul sent out workers to plant churches in the surrounding towns and cities; so the whole province of Asia Minor (modern Turkey) heard the gospel while Paul was at Ephesus.[8] Gary has a vision to reach Indianapolis, a city of 835,000 people. He also wants to spark disciple-making movements in other US cities and around the world. His title may be pastor, but Gary has gone beyond that role. He is a movement pioneer.

GIVE US AUSTIN OR WE DIE!

In 1999 Fred Campbell started a business in underwater video, sonar and acoustic positioning systems in Austin, Texas.[9] The company became a vehicle for ministry to employees, customers and vendors. The Campbells looked for signs of spiritual interest in all the people they met. Many of those people came to Christ and were plugged into local churches.

That wasn't enough for Fred and Melissa. They loved visiting communities and sharing Christ. When knocking on doors, they found that about one in twenty people they talked to would receive Christ. Yet when people came to faith and joined the church, they did not reproduce other disciples.

God gave Fred and Melissa a growing desire to see their city reached for Christ. They began to pray, "Change us. God, give us Austin or we die!"

The Campbells began visiting homes on Saturday mornings. After introducing themselves, Fred and Melissa would say, "We care about you. Here's a free breakfast," and offer them breakfast burritos.[10] Doors would open. Conversations would begin. Then Fred and Melissa would ask, "If God could do a miracle to meet a need you have right now, what would that need be, and could we pray that for you right now?" Nearly half of the people would share a need and receive prayer.

When they made follow-up visits, the Campbells were often welcomed and invited in by those who remembered the first visit. Then in the living room, or sometimes on the front porch, Fred and Melissa would share the story of the woman who wept at Jesus' feet. They asked their hosts to retell the story in their own words, and they talked about it. Then the Campbells shared their stories and the gospel story, using 2 Corinthians 5:17-21.

Finally, Fred or Melissa would ask, "Does this make sense to you?" and follow up with "Is there any reason why you wouldn't want to receive God's gift of forgiveness?" If the person was ready, they led him or her to Christ and made a time to return for foundational discipleship using the series of studies called "Seven Commands of Christ": repent and believe, be baptized, pray, make disciples, love, celebrate the Lord's Supper and give generously.[11] Fred and Melissa found that 80 percent of people who welcomed their return visit would either accept Christ or ask them to come back again so they could hear another story.

The Campbells trained others to do what they do, but they weren't seeing multiplication. Then, in February 2013 they met Jeff Sundell. Through Jeff's training, God filled in the missing pieces. Fred and Melissa knew how to do evangelism, but they wanted to multiply disciples and mobilize them to share the gospel. They heard answers to the questions they were asking:

- Who should we tell?
- What should we say?
- How do we make disciples?
- How do we train disciples in the short term and long term?
- How do we group together new believers?
- How do we grow workers and multiply them?

They exchanged their *evangelistic strategy* for a *discipleship movement strategy*. They began passing on to others what Jeff taught them.

In April of 2013, after mapping the greater Austin area into regions, the Campbells sent out their first forty two–member teams to search for receptive "houses of peace" in twelve areas.[12] They found four hundred houses of peace and formed more than sixty new groups within sixty days of this first search. Additional searches in August and November identified 150 more potential houses of peace. By December 2013 they had more than one hundred groups meeting.

During this time Fred and Melissa took a local pastor along to help with follow-up visits. In the first home a mother came to Christ. In the next home a man wasn't ready to receive Christ, so they asked, "Can we come back next week and tell you another story?" He replied, "Yes! You would do that?"

In the third home they visited, they met a Christian Iranian man who had just arrived in Austin the night before. In Iran he had been imprisoned and tortured for a year. He told the Campbells, "Last night, I dreamed someone was knocking on my door. I came and opened the door, but no one was there, so I went back to sleep. A few hours later, I had the same dream, so again I came downstairs. And here you are!" On the plane he had prayed, "Jesus, I will suffer more for you, or do whatever you want me to do, but will you please give me at least one friend in the US?"

Later that day, this man went with Fred and the pastor as they visited his new community. He watched them bring an entire household to Christ. He was overjoyed, and his home became the base for reaching that community.

The pastor accompanying Fred and Melissa was stunned. He asked, "How many people have you seen come to Christ here?" Fred told him there were over sixty in this one housing development. The pastor said, "We could plant a church here right now!" So they did. This church began meeting outdoors in July 2013. Before this church begins a worship service, the believers walk through the community with guitars, singing and inviting people to join them.

The members of this new church wondered what they could do for their community. They saw a fallen fence that needed to be fixed in order to deter children from wandering toward a major highway. So they asked the management of this 420-unit complex if they could pay to fix the fence.

The management committee was so impressed that they told the church members, "Do anything you want here, just don't amplify with speakers." By October 2013 the gathering grew to more than one hundred adults and fifty children. At Thanksgiving, with no outside assistance, the new believers organized and funded a feast for all the community residents.

When the church gathers, they worship and pray for each other. There's loving accountability as they ask, "Have you obeyed what you learned last week? Have you been fishing for new disciples?"

Fred and Melissa offered to train them in reaching their community and going into unreached communities. Twenty-six people from the one apartment complex turned up for training. And churches are starting in other neighborhoods. Most of them begin with four to six people and then move outdoors when they grow beyond twelve to fifteen people.

According to Fred, this is happening in twenty-eight communities. Some are middle class, some are working poor, others are in the projects, where many people live with government assistance. Everywhere the church members go they find households of peace who open the door to the gospel. Even in traditionally resistant areas, almost half the people they meet welcome a return visit to hear a story of hope and the gospel. In the suburbs two-thirds respond positively.

Fred and Melissa now have a simple and reproducible way to enter a new community. They have an effective way to present the gospel, which can be quickly passed on to trainees.

In 2014 Fred and Melissa began partnering with local churches in Austin to send out one hundred teams each month to identify ten thousand potential "houses of peace." They support similar efforts in Houston and other US cities. One of those cities is San Antonio.

CHUCK WOOD'S VISION FOR SAN ANTONIO

When Chuck Wood came to Christ, he instinctively knew he needed to share his newfound faith. By 2010 he had been making disciples for thirty years and was serving on a national leadership level with the Military Mission of the Navigators.[13]

The book *Movements That Change the World* launched Chuck into a three-year journey to learn what God was doing around the world through disciple-making movements. He felt God was challenging him to leave his position with the Navigators and head back to grassroots discipleship. He would reevaluate everything he knew about ministry and start with a clean slate. For the next year Chuck devoured every book on movements, discipleship, church planting and missionary biographies he could find. Through Henry Blackaby's *Experiencing God*, Chuck rediscovered the principle of joining God in the work he is already doing (John 5:19-20).

Then for six months Chuck put the books aside and only read the Bible. He devoted hours to prayer each day. He studied Luke and Acts. Chuck was desperate to see movements multiplying in the United States, just as they were in other parts of the world.

The Holy Spirit led Chuck and Deb Wood to move to San Antonio. They developed a disciple-making ministry there, as they had always done for the last thirty years. But they knew something had to be different if they were to see a movement. People were coming to faith in San Antonio, but they weren't passing on their faith to others. Three different new believers told Chuck that what he did was too hard and too complicated for them to copy.

December 2012 was a turning point. Chuck read the book *T4T: Discipleship Re-Revolution* by Steve Smith and Ying Kai. As he began to read, Chuck heard a voice in his heart say, "Humble yourself and do this." Chuck had read hundreds of books on discipleship. He wasn't about to drop everything he knew and blindly start doing what the latest book taught. But the voice would not go away, and finally he accepted that it was the Holy Spirit.

The next section he read was about answering the question, What would it take? For Chuck, that meant asking, What would it take to reach San Antonio for Christ? Metropolitan San Antonio has a population of 2.3 million people. The vision Chuck received was for 2,020 disciple-making groups or churches by the year 2020. His first reaction was that this vision statement sounded too cheesy! But he couldn't let it go.

Chuck took what he had learned from Steve Smith and Ying Kai and began applying it. A new believer Chuck trained started his own discipleship group in Fort Sam Houston and went from five to thirty-five people in three weeks. He led several people to Christ in the following weeks. New disciples began leading Discovery Bible Studies for friends and family. Chuck now had a method of making disciples that was rapidly reproducing.

After twelve months, at the end of 2013, Chuck and Deb's two discipleship groups had grown to seventeen groups. They baptized nine people and trained twenty-eight people to lead discipleship groups. By 2014 they had three generations of groups and four generations of new disciples.

Chuck has a vision for reaching the whole city. So he's reached out to church planters and traditional churches to cast vision for San Antonio and to train them and their people. He walks trainees through the Gospels to discover how Jesus entered into a lost community, shared the gospel, made disciples, developed community and reproduced the next generation of workers. Chuck teaches people to do what Jesus did.

Chuck trained Grace Community Church, which became a training hub that planned to start churches throughout the city. They didn't care if the churches were in coffee shops, restaurants or homes—they wanted to reach the city.

Chuck has also been training others around the United States and internationally. Because Chuck has been diagnosed with ALS (Lou Gehrig's disease), much of his training is through video conferencing. Chuck's trainees from across six countries have planted twenty-two churches and started 106 discipleship groups. There are sixty second-generation groups and churches, and fourteen third-generation groups and churches. Two hundred and fifty-two people who were far from God are now engaged in disciple-making groups and churches. Chuck and Deb continue to serve with NavNeighbors, a ministry of the Navigators.

THE 50-5-50 VISION

While all this was unfolding, Jeff Sundell's vision for America was taking shape. He did some research and discovered that within a decade 187 American cities will be majority-minority cities—the majority of citizens will be non-European and non–African American. The majority would come from the minority—from Asia, Africa, the Middle East and Latin America. One of those top ten majority-minority cities is Charlotte, North Carolina, near Jeff's home. Charlotte's schools reflect the changing makeup of the city. Students come from three to four hundred people groups and speak 216 languages.

Jeff's vision has been shaped by the changing face of America. His 50-5-50 Vision is aimed to reach fifty majority-minority US cities in five years (2013–2017).[14] What does *reached* look like? Jeff used to count numbers of conversions, baptisms, groups started and churches started. Not anymore. Now he tracks generational streams of church planting.

In every city he wants to see multiple streams of new churches that typically reach at least the fourth generation; that is, a church of new disciples plants a church, and that new church plants a church, and that newest church plants a church.

To reach fifty cities in five years, Jeff needs fifty fourth-generation (4G) trainers in each city. Each 4G trainer has produced at least one stream of fourth-generation churches and is training others to do the same.

Does this sound like Jeff's dreaming? There are now thirteen cities with at least one 4G trainer. Seven cities have fourth-generation churches. Another fourteen cities have second- and third-generation discipleship groups.

Jeff's goal is "no place left," fifty cities with fifty fourth-generation trainers in five years.

eight

From Church to Movement

*An unchurchly mission is as much a
monstrosity as an unmissionary church.*

Lesslie Newbigin, *The Household of God*

Qwesi Young of Ghana leads a small church of African immigrants in Charlotte, North Carolina: Global Harvest Family Church International.[1] Qwesi wants to make disciples and plant churches in West Africa and the United States. He invited Jeff Sundell to help them get started. Soon the Wednesday night prayer meetings became training time in making disciples. They learned the basics of how to share their stories and how to share God's story. They learned how to find people of peace.

Global Harvest, a church of African immigrants, is in an African American community. The cultural divide between the two groups is huge. Qwesi remembers how scared he was the first time they went into their community. As he approached a group of young African American males with their dreadlocks and intimidating looks, he knew he couldn't back down. After all, he was the pastor and his people were watching!

Qwesi went up to the group, introduced himself and asked, "If God could do a miracle in your life today, what would it be? And can I pray for you?" To his amazement two of the men wanted prayer. One was looking for work. The other recently had a blowup with his girlfriend. Qwesi prayed for them and shared his story of meeting Jesus. He told the men how they too could know Jesus. As they listened, Qwesi told them the story of the woman who wept at Jesus' feet (Luke 7:36-50). That night two people agreed to open up their homes to a Discovery Bible Study.

One evening Qwesi was visiting the African American community when he met one of the young men, Ace, from the first encounter. Ace told Qwesi that since they first met he could not get Qwesi's story out of his mind. Ace and his girlfriend, Taheeda, gave their lives to Christ that night.

Qwesi and others from the church kept returning to "love loud," as Qwesi calls it. They shared gifts of food, prayed for needs, shared the gospel and launched Discovery Bible Studies in homes. They challenged the new disciples to be the answer to reaching their own community.

Wednesday nights have become the highlight in the church's week. One Wednesday night they were visiting a Hispanic community. They arrived to discover that a dispute in an apartment complex had erupted into a mini-riot. Fists were flying; teens, adults and even grandmas were joining in the fight.

The police arrived and closed down the area. Qwesi and his team could not leave. So they began moving among people, asking the miracle question—"If God could do a miracle in your life today, what would it be? How can we pray for you?"

Late that night, they returned to the church to debrief. Qwesi told the story of how the gospel came to his community in Ghana. First, the German and Swiss missionaries arrived, but they soon died from tropical diseases. So others came and died. Still others came. They didn't give up and just kept coming, sharing the gospel and teaching people how to follow Jesus. They won his grandfather to Christ, and he became a key leader. Then Qwesi announced, "That's what we're going to do! We will keep going to this community. One African, two Africans—whatever it takes, we will not stop!"

WAITING FOR GOD IN THE CAPE TOWN AIRPORT

In 2009 David Broodryk flew into the Cape Town airport, got off the plane, walked into the terminal, sat down and waited. He had no idea who or what he was waiting for. He ordered a coffee and opened his computer.[2] David asked the Lord, "What should I do? Where should I go?" No clear answer came.

Because movements move, David had been moving around South Africa looking for signs of where God was at work. That's why he was in the Cape Town airport that day, drinking coffee. Waiting. He had no leads in Cape Town.

As he waited, he checked his email. He had no contacts in Cape Town, but an email arrived from someone in Cape Town who found him online and wanted to connect and talk about disciple-making movements. He replied, "I'm in Cape Town, not far from you. Can I come over?"

From that time David began building a network of people in Cape Town. Many of them were ordinary believers weary of how their churches had become stagnant and ingrown. He began training them in the basics of disciple-making movements.

On his third trip to Cape Town one of the participants mentioned that she had grown up with the leader of one of the largest churches in the city—Peter Snyman of The Lighthouse. She wondered if David would like to meet Peter, but David wasn't interested. He'd already given up on trying to recruit existing churches to transition to disciple-making movements. She persisted, and eventually he agreed to one meeting.

David discovered that Peter Snyman was also frustrated and discontent. Lighthouse had a history of pioneering change. In the dark days of apartheid, Lighthouse was one of the first churches in South Africa to open its doors to all races. God gave the church a heart to reach the nations. Peter understood that a large, institutionalized church with facilities and staff was not going to reproduce in the parts of the world that were least reached. Something had to be different. Yet, despite the best intentions and many attempts, Lighthouse wasn't able to turn into reality the vision God gave them.

The meeting went well, but it didn't lead immediately to anything. A year later David was back in Cape Town training when the same woman approached him and said, "You need to meet with Peter again." At the same time God had been speaking to David about having the faith to believe that disciple-making movements could happen through existing churches.

Soon David was sitting in Peter's office. Peter was frank; he didn't believe The Lighthouse could adopt a disciple-making movement strategy. The church had tried so many different approaches, and they were now weary of attempts to introduce change that did not gain traction.

David wasn't taking a step back. He knew God was in this. He told Peter, "You're wrong, and I'll tell you why." Over the next hour David painted a picture of how the church could look beyond its own four walls and reach the whole city of Cape Town. He went into the meeting without a clear plan, but as they talked, a strategy emerged that would change a church that would change a city.

Peter's attention was captured by the simple method of Discovery Bible Study as the lynchpin for a disciple-making movement. Finally, he had a handle on a process that was doable. Peter bought in. In November 2010 David met with the pastors and elders of The Lighthouse and shared the vision for disciple-making movements.

David knew that while key leaders with existing commitments may not be the early adopters of disciple-making movements, they are the gateway to early adopters who are ready for action. Most early adopters are frustrated with the lack of progress in making disciples. They also frustrate the leadership of the church. Most church leaders are working to maintain the stability of their churches. The last thing they want is for someone to come in and create chaos.

So David trained the senior leaders and elders of the church, including the church's founders—Peter Snyman's parents. By the end of the training the leadership agreed to offer the training to a wider group of leaders and influencers. Finally, David returned for a third training early in 2011, to which the whole church was invited. Two thousand people had a taste of the training in a church service. Three hundred people participated in the full training.

The purpose of the training was to find people who were ready for action, form them into teams, help them get started and assist them in bringing others onboard. David wanted to mobilize them to reach people in the community the church would never reach.

The training helped build churchwide ownership. It also surfaced early adopters. David has trained over thirty thousand people, and he says he still can't predict who is ready to implement the process. He has to train and watch for the people who make a start.

David formed a mentoring relationship with Peter and made a two-year commitment to help the church implement disciple-making movements. The Cape Town airport became a regular destination as David trained the church leadership in the values and practices of disciple-making movements. They took what they were learning and worked it into the life of the church. David believes it's important to walk with everyone through the transition. Failure to do this can divide the church

Change still came at a price. Not everyone embraced disciple-making movements. Some were cautious; others were resistant. The Lighthouse leadership knew that not everybody would be ready to go into the community and make disciples. They sought other ways to help them contribute to the vision for disciple-making movements.

The Lighthouse leadership released the early adopters to share the gospel, to make disciples and to train others. Some dropped whatever they were doing and devoted themselves to multiplying disciples. Peter set up a pioneer team of early adopters from among the staff, interns and the congregation. Soon reports were coming back to the church. People's resistance and indifference melted as they began hearing stories of lives changed by the gospel.

The entire church didn't move outside the walls of the building. But the entire church became supportive of disciple-making movements. In the first phase, Discovery Bible Study groups began spreading throughout the church. Next, people started Discovery Bible Studies with friends and family who were far from God. Finally, they began reaching people of peace among groups that had no relational link with church members.

Teams started outreaches to Somali refugees, prostitutes, drug addicts and gang members. All of these groups were unlikely to step inside the door of Lighthouse. Now they were coming to Christ through Discovery Bible Study, forming into groups and growing in discipleship.

The simplicity of Discovery Bible Study groups meant the groups could spread to new communities. Lighthouse began groups among farm laborers in a community over an hour from Cape Town. Soon disciples were walking in oppressive heat to pioneer new groups among other farm laborers. A local farmer offered to transport them, but the disciples declined. They wanted to take responsibility for the spread of the groups. Newly formed churches were led and financed by farm laborers.

In 2010 South Africa hosted the Soccer World Cup. Before the event the homeless were rounded up and placed in a shack town called Blikkiesdorp (Tin Can Town). Lighthouse people and a coalition of disciple makers from Cape Town began walking the rows of one-room shacks, looking for people of peace, which they found within a half hour. They formed discipleship groups in the community.

When the World Cup ended, the inhabitants of Tin Can Town slowly returned to their original communities. Soon there were disciples reproducing in those communities.

An eight-year-old girl from Lighthouse watched as her father facilitated Discovery Bible Studies. She announced, "I can do this!" She lived in a rough part of Cape Town known for its

gangs, so she began working with the children at the local park.
Two years later she was still making disciples. She attends the
Lighthouse leaders' gathering and sometimes brings her dis-
ciples with her.

Meanwhile, Lighthouse members formed Discovery Bible
Study groups in their workplaces. Some of those groups, started
by a high-ranking female police officer, took hold in the police
headquarters.

Peter can't keep track of all the groups that have started. He
just counts the groups where Lighthouse has a direct mentoring
relationship, which numbers around 180. Some of them are
third- and fourth-generation groups.

As momentum built David Broodryk decided to make Peter
an offer, "I'll stop all my training and coaching in Cape Town
and work solely with you and Lighthouse on one condition. You
take what you've learned and give it away to the city's churches."

Snyman agreed and committed to build a coalition of
churches pursuing disciple-making movements in Cape Town.
They meet monthly and share struggles, challenges, lessons and
breakthroughs. They hold each other accountable for what they
will do next. They identify unreached areas and people groups
in the city and form teams to reach them.

Today David rarely visits Cape Town. Peter and Lighthouse
have accepted the challenge of mobilizing all of God's people to
reach the city. Movements multiply. David's work has multiplied
at every level in Cape Town—disciple makers, church planters,
trainers, mentors, movement catalysts. His job is finished.
Peter is now David's peer in training and coaching leaders for
disciple-making movements. Movements move. It was time for
David to move on.

FROM MEGACHURCH TO MOVEMENT CATALYST

Everything is bigger in Texas, especially its churches. Sugar Creek Baptist is a megachurch of four thousand people on the outskirts of Houston. The nations have come to Houston, which is located in Fort Bend County. Fort Bend is one of a growing number of counties where the majority of people are from ethnic minorities.[3]

Don Waybright is the missions pastor at Sugar Creek. His mission focus is both local and global. Outside the United States, the church is a catalyst for movements in Honduras, Peru, along the Amazon River in Colombia and in north India.

Houston has a significant refugee population of Burmese, Bhutanese and Nepali refugees. So Don invited the Keystone Project to send a team of missionaries to reach those communities.[4] Sugar Creek provided financial and logistical support, and encouraged its members to get involved.

There are fifty thousand refugees who live in several blocks of high density, multilevel housing. The team moved into the community and began engaging people from Hindu, Muslim and Buddhist backgrounds. Around three hundred people have come to know Christ. There are multiple streams of fourth-generation disciples and six healthy new churches. One of them is a second-generation church.

Why not just enfold the people into the existing church at Sugar Creek? There are practical reasons regarding language and transportation. But the most important reason is that Don wants to see new believers taking responsibility to form churches in their communities and reproduce them in unreached communities.

There's another missional initiative at the University of Houston. Sugar Creek planted a church there as an incubator for

church-planting movements. The church is reaching students
and mobilizing them for mission beyond the university. Right
next to the university is the Third Ward, one of the six historic
wards of Houston. It's a marginalized community of African
Americans and home to some of the most dangerous neighborhoods in the country. Students are now making disciples and
planting first- and second-generation churches in Third Ward.
Sugar Creek has released one of their staff to lead the work.

Disciples are being made at the university, among refugees
and in impoverished communities. Inmates are reproducing disciples and simple churches within the prison system around
Houston, as well. There is a multiplication stream in the Dar-
rington Maximum Security Prison that is so effective that prison
authorities asked it to be reproduced in all twenty-six prisons
around Houston.

In the suburbs Sugar Creek is training young families to
reach their communities. They want to multiply new groups in
new housing developments and hope these groups will remain
connected with the life of the central church at Sugar Creek.

Don participates in learning communities for practitioners
and increasingly sends out trainers from Sugar Creek to equip
other churches around the nation.

REWRITING THE JOB DESCRIPTION
TO FIT THE VISION

Most churches are not ready to embrace disciple-making movements. Some churches can't make the full transition but are
willing to support church planters or crosscultural workers who
are. Other churches are ready to send a team into their communities to start disciple-making movements.

One such church is Crossway, a church of four thousand in Melbourne, Australia. I came to faith at Crossway. Michelle and I led the team that planted Crossway's first new church. Crossway continues to plant churches and form new congregations. It has sent out and supports over fifty missionaries around the world. In the last few years it has helped start a new mission entity called Praxeis, which is focused on disciple-making movements.[5]

The story of Praxeis began when Dave Lawton, a senior leader at Crossway, and his wife, Colleen, began using their days off to walk the streets of the western suburbs of Melbourne, praying and looking for persons of peace. They found them, and soon were in homes leading Discovery Bible Studies. So Dave went back to the church and explained that he could not keep up with his responsibilities as a Crossway pastor and continue his work in Melbourne's western suburbs.

For many churches this would have meant that Dave should resign. Instead, Dale Stephenson, Crossway's senior pastor, rewrote Dave's job description to match the unfolding vision to multiply disciples. Then Crossway reshaped its church-planting priorities, from planting traditional churches, which grew through transfers, to sparking disciple-making movements.

Soon others joined Dave and Colleen, and Praxeis grew. Dave's vision stretched beyond the western suburbs of Melbourne to the nation of Australia. He and other Praxeis workers began walking the cities and towns of the nation, praying and looking for people of peace.

Meanwhile, Crossway provided logistical and financial support while Praxeis was forming. They provided oversight and accountability for Dave. Some Crossway members and staff joined Praxeis with their church's blessing.

Rather than see this new mission as a threat that would deprive them of funds and people, Crossway embraced what God was doing and formed a partnership with Praxeis. The relationship continues today as Praxeis now has its own governing board, organizational structure and sources of funding. It has become an independent entity in partnership with Crossway and other churches. There are now over 150 Praxeis volunteers across Australia. Twelve of them have raised their missionary support and are full time. Praxeis has overseas workers in Hungary and Spain, with plans for a team in Japan.

BECOMING A GREAT COMMISSION CHURCH

Between AD 52 and 55, Paul spent three years in the city of Ephesus, a major city of the Roman Empire of around 200,000 people. It was the capital of the Roman province of Asia (modern-day Turkey).

By the end of his stay, Luke tells us, "all the Jews and Greeks who lived in the province of Asia heard the word of the Lord" (Acts 19:10). At this time the population of Asia Minor was at least ten million people.

Paul did not take the gospel to the whole province of Asia on his own. He was based in Ephesus, where he was teaching every day. Epaphras established churches in the neighboring cities of Laodicea, Hierapolis and Colossae in the Lycos Valley (Colossians 1:3-8; 2:1; 4:13). No doubt Paul trained and sent others throughout Asia Minor. To the north, the churches in the cities of Smyrna, Pergamum, Thyatira, Sardis and Philadelphia, referred to in Revelation 2–3, could also have been started around this time. For centuries the region was one of the leading centers of Christianity.

A Great Commission church

Paul planted a church—a Great Commission church—in Ephesus that sparked a movement. A Great Commission church wants to reach their community, not just grow their church. A Great Commission church gives away people and resources to pioneer movements in unreached fields beyond their community.

Existing churches can and do act as catalysts for movements. But there is nothing automatic or predictable in the journey. Each story has something different to teach us. The following are some recurring themes.

A Great Commission church has to be a work of God. The best we can do in managing change and training is not enough. God has to link the right people at the right time. He must initiate and sustain the work.

God often uses movement pioneers from outside the church as change agents. Their job is to (1) feed discontent with the status quo, (2) cast a vision of what God could do, and (3) provide simple but profound methods to get people started and help them remain on track.

We have to get the right people on the bus. Every church has formal leaders and people of influence who need to own the transition. The vision has to be clear, but the church will need to go on a journey to embrace it. That journey can be painful.

One movement catalyst told me how he clashed with his senior pastor over the direction they were headed. The next day the senior pastor told him, "I've been doing this job for over thirty years. I know how to lead this church. But I don't understand your language. Still, I want you to keep speaking that language and don't stop." That took humility and courage to say.

Once key leaders are onboard with the direction, training in making disciples has to be rolled out for as many people as possible. A least *three touches* are needed—three experiences of training within six months. Following each training, there must be opportunities for disciples to put it into practice.

For those who are willing, it's important for an experienced trainer to take them into the community to find people of peace. That means meeting people, offering to pray for needs and sharing with them. The goal is to find a home that is ready to host a Discovery Bible Study.

Most people, including church leaders, will find this prospect terrifying. Yet God will work through their weaknesses to do amazing things in people's lives. Disciples who look for people of peace often return rejoicing at having seen the power of God. The experience changes them.

Many, if not most, of the people are not ready to implement what they have learned in training immediately. It's important not to force them but to help them find ways that can contribute to making disciples. It's better not to force the vision on them, but shift the focus to the life-changing gospel.

A smaller group will begin to orient their lives and ministries around multiplying disciples. These early adopters—and you can't predict who they will be—are key to the transition. To build momentum and lock in change, vision has to be validated by action. The stories of what God is doing in people's lives will build faith and provide an answer for critics.

Once the early adopters are identified, it's important to form them into teams for frequent encouragement and accountability. They meet monthly for ninety minutes to answer four questions.

1. What has God been doing (reproducing gospel, reproducing discipleship, reproducing church formation)?

2. Where are you stuck (reproducing gospel, reproducing discipleship, reproducing church formation)?

3. What two things do you need to do to move toward generational growth?

4. How can we pray for you?

The team(s) of early adopters soon become(s) the trainers and coaches of others in the church. Twice a year they meet with other practitioners for mid-level training. Each team reports and works through the same four questions in depth. Together they learn and apply the principles of disciple-making movements with an experienced facilitator.

A Great Commission church will work on a number of fronts.

1. It equips every believer to follow Jesus in loving obedience and to fish for people. It teaches everyone who wants to learn how to lead a Discovery Bible Study, share his or her story, share God's story and pray for needs. The goal is making disciples who are growing in obedience to Christ's commands and reaching those with whom they have relations.

2. It mobilizes teams to seek people of peace locally in unreached communities and people groups. The teams meet monthly in an iron-on-iron meeting and twice a year for mid-level training.

3. Its end vision is the formation of multiple streams of four generations of discipleship groups and churches in its community and in the unreached fields God has called it to.

4. It partners with mission agencies to send workers into unreached fields beyond its reach.

5. It equips other churches through training and coaching to become Great Commission churches.

If becoming a Great Commission church is beyond your reach, remember pastor Qwesi and Global Harvest. If a church of forty African immigrants from twenty-two nations can become a Great Commission church, there's hope for you.

nine
·····

No Place Left in the House of Islam

A wind is blowing through the House of Islam.

David Garrison

Hussain tours villages on his 125cc scooter looking for Muslims who want to learn more about *Isa* (Arabic for Jesus).[1] When he finds someone who is willing to listen, Hussain asks the person to gather friends and family to hear about Isa and decide whether they want to follow him. He has found that one of the best places to meet people is in the local teahouse. In one village Hussain noticed a man in the teahouse to whom everyone paid respect. Some feared him. Sadik was the local moneylender. Every day while he sat and drank tea, desperate people would come to him for money. Some trembled as they explained why they couldn't pay. Sadik was a violent man. The villagers were right to fear him.

Through Hussain, Sadik and his family became followers of Isa. Everyone in the village, including Sadik's family, noticed the transformation. Sadik led Nazir, the herbalist, to follow Isa.

Through Nazir, Sumon, a farmer, and all his relatives began following Isa. Sumon began discovery groups with other farming families.

Hussain trains these new *Isahi* (disciples of Jesus) to plant an Isa *jamaat* (gathering) in every town and village. Hussain has a "no place left" vision for every one of his nation's villages. At last count two thousand villages now have an Isa jamaat.

Within a century of Muhammad's death in AD 632 Arab armies had defeated both the Byzantine and Persian empires, and subjugated tens of millions of Christians to Islamic rule. For over one thousand years the Islamic faith spread from the deserts of the Middle East to capture the loyalty of over 1.6 billion people today.[2] *Dar al-Islam* (House of Islam) is the name Muslims give to the spiritual empire that stretches from the west coast of Africa to the islands of Indonesia. It is made up of forty-nine Muslim-majority nations.

Not until the nineteenth century was the first voluntary movement of Muslims to Christ recorded. By the twentieth century there had been thirteen Muslim movements to Christ. Today a shift has occurred. In the first twelve years of the twenty-first century David Garrison has identified sixty-nine new Muslim movements to Christ in twenty-nine nations scattered throughout sub-Saharan Africa, the Arab world, the Persian world, Central Asia, South Asia and Southeast Asia (see fig. 9.1).[3]

THE QUR'AN AS A BRIDGE

Amid Hasan is a devout Sunni Muslim from India.[4] As a young man he served in the Merchant Marines. He devoted himself to read the Qur'an in Arabic. One day his captain asked him if he understood the meaning of what he was reading. He had to admit that although he could read Arabic, he didn't understand it. His captain laughed and said that was the stupidest thing he'd ever heard. At first Amid was furious, but eventually he wondered if the captain was right.

When he returned from sea Amid bought a copy of the Qur'an in his native Bangla language and began to read. Soon he noticed that there were stories in the Qur'an that contradicted what the *mawlanas*, his Islamic teachers, had taught him.

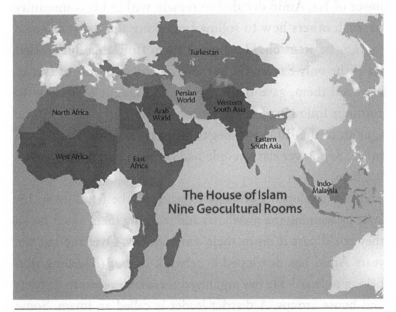

Figure 9.1. Nine geocultural rooms in the House of Islam

He read the Qur'an to learn more about Muhammad, yet it was Isa (Jesus) who drew his attention.

As Amid read the Qur'an he discovered that it elevated Isa above Muhammad. He learned that the Qur'an gave Isa twenty-three titles of honor, yet none for Muhammad. Isa is with Allah in heaven, Muhammad is not with Allah now. Isa will return; Muhammad will not. Isa is alive; Muhammad is dead. The Qur'an speaks of Isa ninety-seven times, only four times does it mention Muhammad. Isa's name means Savior; Muhammad is not a savior. Isa is called *Ruhullah*, the Spirit of Allah. Muhammad is only a messenger.

Amid began to debate with the mawlanas, challenging them to obey the Qur'an and follow Isa. He obtained a Bible and began reading about Jesus. After being baptized as a follower of Isa, Amid decided to remain within his community to teach others how to follow Isa, taking them on the same journey he went on. He showed them from the Qur'an that Isa is the only Savior. Once they became followers of Isa, he baptized them, gave them a Bible and taught them how to continue following Isa. With time they moved away from the Qur'an to the Bible and began helping others come to faith in Isa. Soon over sixty people had come to faith and received baptism.

Amid developed a strategy to reach all the Muslims in his state by winning the mawlanas and teaching them about Isa so they could pass it on to their communities. Over the last ten years Amid has developed a network of *Isai* (Muslims who belong to Jesus). He has organized these believers into districts and house groups. A district leader is called an imam. Some imams are responsible for several hundred jamaats. Each jamaat is led by a *rabbur* ("one who shows the way").

The strategy is simple, the Qur'an is a bridge to discovering Isa in the *Injil* (The Gospels). In Amid's network there are about three thousand Isa jamaats with thirty thousand Muslims who follow Isa.

FINDING THE RIGHT PEOPLE, HELPING THEM DISCOVER JESUS

Jerry Trousdale has identified three ways gospel ambassadors find persons of peace among Muslims.[5]

Acts of kindness. A key is finding ways to express love to a Muslim community or family. Compassion opens the door to relationship. It may be a simple project like providing a seedbed to grow food. For example, in one Muslim village, before a crop was planted, believers gathered their new Muslim friends and prayed that God would provide the largest harvest they had ever seen. God has even used forgiveness in the face of persecution to transform a persecutor's heart.

Prayer with power. Intercessory prayer prepares the way for the gospel. Often God's power is revealed through dreams and visions that point to Jesus or his messengers. In other cases people are healed of physical ailments or delivered of demonic oppression. In a drought-stricken village a messenger began walking the dry lake bed and praying for rain. After the rain came the people were ready to hear what he had to share.

Looking for God-prepared people. God-prepared people already live in many Muslim communities. They are waiting for the right person to come along and help them find answers to their questions. The only way to find these seekers is through prayer and presence among Muslims. As the story of Amid Hasan shows, breakthroughs come when a seeker is also a person of influence in the community.

The role of the ambassador is to identify the person of peace and help that person and their friends and family discover Jesus in the Bible. Together the group learns to follow and obey Jesus as the Holy Spirit speaks through the Word. The ambassador is

a coach and a catalyst as God's Word transforms people and a
new community of disciples emerges.

THE WIDOW AND THE BLIND MAN

Mama Nadirah is an amazing woman God is using to pioneer
movements among Muslims.[6] She grew up as a Muslim but
married a Christian. She never received a formal education and
could not read or write. As others read her the Bible, Nadirah
began to memorize it. Her son Joseph introduced her to the principles of disciple-making movements, and she learned that God
could use ordinary people to make disciples and plant churches.

Nadirah, a woman of prayer, lived to introduce her Muslim
friends to a life in the presence of God. Sadly, her husband died,
but this did not dampen her resolve to reach Muslims. She
opened her home to anyone in need of prayer, healing, counsel
and love. Before long God had given her a new family of people
who were following Jesus.

Zamil was a successful and influential business leader. He was
a respected man at his mosque. One night, *Isa al-Masih* (Jesus
the Messiah) appeared to him in a dream and revealed that he
(Isa) is the Light of the world. When Zamil awoke, he discovered that he was blind.

Eventually, Zamil was invited to a prayer camp run by Mama
Nadirah. There he received prayer, but his sight did not return.
Nevertheless, he gave his life to Jesus. His family rejected him,
and he lost everything.

Through Mama Nadirah Zamil began attending Discovery
Bible Studies and learning how to follow Jesus. He decided he
would obey Christ's command and go into the villages to make
disciples. Nadirah gently reminded him that he was blind. That

did not deter him. Without telling anyone, he hired a taxi and drove to a Muslim village God had placed on his heart. Here was a blind man searching for a person of peace.

A month later Zamil called Mama Nadirah to inform her that he was coming home now that he had successfully planted a church in the community. He returned home for a short time and went to another village. Six weeks later it too had a church of new disciples. A blind man discipled by an illiterate widow is planting churches in Muslim villages. ⁱ

Mama Nadirah and the believers with her are committed to planting churches throughout their nation and the Muslim world. She is mobilizing, training and coaching men and women to pray for this impossible goal, to make disciples and to plant churches. So far, more than four thousand new churches have been established in five nations. Eight of those churches were started by a blind man named Zamil.

A JOURNEY OF DISCOVERY AND OBEDIENCE

It is important to start with the right people. Too often ministries among Muslims begin with people who are disconnected from their community. They are snapped up and added to the Christian community and the spread of the gospel ends with them. The key to a movement is that it begins with seekers who are strongly integrated into their community. When they become disciples they stay within their community as persons of influence.

Often the starting point is not the Bible but the Qur'an. The Qur'an cannot lead a person to faith in Christ, but it can serve as a bridge to discovering Christ in the Scriptures. The Qur'an has more to say about Isa al-Masih than it has to say about

Muhammad. From the Qur'an a Muslim can learn three things about Isa:

1. *Isa is holy.* The Qur'an describes Isa as the word of Allah (God), the Ruhullah (Spirit of God) and the Messiah whose name means "Savior." He is righteous and born of a virgin.

2. *Isa is powerful.* He gave sight to the blind, healed lepers and raised the dead. It is a Muslim's duty to Allah to obey Isa. To know what Isa commands us to do, we must read the *Injil.*

3. *Isa knows the way to heaven.* Allah raised Isa to himself. Isa is in heaven and knows the way to heaven. Those who follow Isa are above those who disbelieve.[7]

A person of peace will heed the Qur'an's instruction to learn from what Muslims call "the former books," that is, the Bible.[8] The next step is to begin a journey of discovering God in the Bible with their family and friends. The place to begin is with the story of creation and move through portions of the Old Testament, such as the prophets of the Old Testament, before moving on to the stories about Jesus in the Gospels.[9] These are discovery groups, not teaching sessions. The messenger must have confidence in the power of God's Word and the work of the Holy Spirit as these groups gather to learn.

Another essential element is that the groups are obedience oriented. Through reading and obeying God's Word together, people are discipled toward conversion. Other elements are prayer and a loving community. As the group learns to follow Christ together, they discover what it means to be his people together. When this occurs, church formation more naturally flows out of discipleship.

When Muslims put their faith in Christ, they discover for

themselves that he commanded them to be baptized, to love one another, to form community or church with other believers, to celebrate the Lord's Supper, to tell others about him and to be faithful when persecuted.

When obedience to the Word of God is central, groups become self-taught and self-correcting. They are readily reproducible with less instruction needed by outsiders. These groups are the building blocks of movements to Christ among Muslim-background believers.

PIONEERING MOVEMENTS AMONG MUSLIMS

What is required of an effective movement pioneer among Muslims? In almost every case the pioneers are Muslim-background believers. In those instances when they are not Muslim-background believers, they have grown up in majority-Muslim environments. Typically they are not cultural outsiders or Westerners attempting to live as insiders. (Although an outsider may make important contributions to their initiation and subsequent development.)

Basir was born to a Christian mother and Muslim father in Southeast Asia.[10] When he was ten his mother died and he went to live with relatives who were fervent Muslims. His mother had left him a Bible, which he continued to read and led him to faith in Christ. As a young man he met other Muslim-background believers in Christ and was baptized. Through them he met some foreign missionaries who had a vision for reaching his Muslim-majority nation: the gospel to every person and a church in every village and people group. He heard God's call to reach his people.

Basir went to his home village determined to lead someone

to Christ that night. That person was a village elder. Ten days later he led a radical Muslim *jihadi* (fighter) to Christ. The three of them banded together. Just six months later, in mid-2010, there were two hundred Muslim-background believers following Jesus. A movement had begun which now has around four thousand groups.

What characterizes Basir? Those close to him would say a willingness to die for his faith. He is both humble and determined. Despite his achievements he remains willing to learn from outside mentors. He has no desire for the limelight or the trappings of leadership. He develops strong leaders who follow his example of servanthood. He leads by influence, not by control.

Basir treats new believers as partners in the movement. Early on he learned that the key to a movement's expansion is to reach people who can reach their community. Intuitively he knows how to find those people and how to equip them. Typically, if he baptizes ten new believers, eight of them will start discipleship groups that become churches.

Basir is an exceptional leader with an exceptional breadth of vision. In that sense he is not easily reproducible. He is able to draw others into that vision so they own it. He transfers responsibility and authority immediately to new believers. He and his leaders equip ordinary people with simple and transferable methods to share the gospel, make disciples and plant churches. Everyone knows what to do and how to do it.

Obviously pioneers like Basir are people of great courage. They or their people may face the threat of death, imprisonment, beatings and being cut off by their families. In one instance a whole movement was shut down when gunmen entered the home of a key leader and threatened to kill his wife and children. The leader reverted to Islam and gave up the names of other leaders in the network.

Persecution, if it is violent and thorough enough, can destroy a movement before it becomes established. Ironically, so can kindness.

Kindness can come in the form of financial support and notoriety among Western Christians. On more than one occasion movements have stalled when well-meaning Westerners have begun channeling money into movements to pay church planters and pastors. With money comes the contamination of foreign influence and dependency. Motives become mixed and a professional class of church leaders emerges. The movement stalls.

Wise and godly movement pioneers do not reject all outside help; they filter it. There are many examples of effective partnerships between a foreign-mission strategist and a movement pioneer among Muslims. Often the movement leader has applied movement principles through a mixture of Scripture reading, intuition, learning and the leading of the Spirit. But they won't get the whole picture on their own. At some point in the process God brings along a key mentor-trainer from outside to help the pioneer clarify thinking, identify obstacles and overcome them.

The outsider may help with funding, but this is limited to help with the cost of training or expenses for workers directly engaged in multiplication across a region. Dependence on outside funding will never produce an indigenous movement.

Usually only the movement pioneer and key leaders know the person providing outside input. This person's story goes largely untold.

WHAT NO ONE EXPECTED, GOD IS DOING

David Garrison took two and a half years to travel 250,000 miles and gather more than one thousand interviews with Muslims who have turned to Christ. He found that Muslims are coming to Christ in unprecedented numbers. Not just individual followers but movements of disciples and churches across the Muslim world—the nine rooms in the House of Islam (see fig. 9.1).

Western Christians are playing a role as catalysts and mentors, but these are indigenous movements predominantly led by movement pioneers with a Muslim background. Muslim-background believers are pioneering movements around the world. Yes, these movements represent only a small percentage of the Muslim world. And, yes, they have their problems, as all movements do. Yet God is doing something truly wonderful.

ten

What Would It Take to Stop You?

> *God, I can't plant churches anymore. I didn't sign on to*
> *love people, train people, send people, and get them killed.*

David Watson, *Contagious Disciple Making*

We all face challenges. Yet it appears that movement pioneers are especially prone to these critical moments when their lives and ministries are on the line.

David Watson had an effective ministry in a Muslim country before he was deported.[1] Undaunted, he moved to India, where he worked hard for three years for very little fruit. Within eighteen months six men Watson had worked alongside were martyred. The Indian government expelled him and his family. More than twenty-five hundred miles separated him from the 80 million Bhojpuri people in north India he was called to reach. Every day for two months David begged God to take away his call to the Bhojpuri and allow him to go home. God would not release him.

Bill Smith has spent many years training and coaching movement pioneers. Many of them have paid a high price. One example he gave was a worker in Asia who faced intense conflict on the team he led. The atmosphere became toxic, and Andrew was forced to leave the field. He returned home deeply troubled. He felt God had abandoned him and that he had no future in ministry. It took years for God to put the pieces back together and bring significant healing. God met him in brokenness, weakness and despair. Eventually, Andrew returned to the field. He saw incredible advances in the spread of the gospel and the multiplication of new churches.

Bill told me, "You know, I've seen plenty of leaders go through this dark night of the soul. Many of them never made it to dawn. They crashed and burned. They gave up the ministry. They lost the vision. They went home and did something different. I've seen there are many more who don't make it through than those who do."

When Bill trains movement pioneers, he reads out a list of challenges they will face, based on actual experiences his trainees have faced over the years. He asks, "Which of these would prevent you from fulfilling your calling?"

1. My spouse decided to call it quits and go home.

2. My parents ordered me to return to my home country.

3. No local school is available for my children.

4. My financial support base is cut by 25 percent.

5. My financial support base is cut by 50 percent.

6. I am diagnosed with a serious degenerative disease.

7. My sending agency collapses.

8. I have to give up home country citizenship in order to do ministry.

9. I am publicly discovered in sin and dismissed by my agency.

10. Some activities essential to evangelization are illegal where my people live.

11. Some activities essential to evangelization are illegal where I reside.

12. My organization supervisor and I strongly disagree on strategy.

13. Others in my organization and I strongly disagree on gifts of the Spirit.

14. I am offered a promotion in my organization involving supervising many field personnel, but no one is left to continue my current work.

15. One of my children is discovered to have leukemia.

16. My spouse dies.

17. One of my children dies.

18. One of my coworkers is killed because of his or her evangelistic work.

19. Someone from my agency that I sent to the field is killed.

20. The first believer from my people group is martyred.

21. All believers in my people group are severely persecuted.

22. My own life will be threatened if I continue this ministry.

23. My spouse's life will be threatened if I continue this ministry.

24. I am offered the pastorate of a large congregation in my home country.

25. After four years there are almost no measurable evangelism results.

This is not an imaginary list. Every one of these events has occurred in the life of one of Bill's friends. Some continued in the ministry, some took this as a sign to give up. Some even gave up on God. Still others chose to move deeper into God.

When God refused to release David Watson from his call, he prayed, "Show me in your Word how you want me to reach these people. If you show me, I will do it."[2] Over the next year God led him through Scripture and opened his eyes. Patterns emerged and new thoughts about church, making disciples and church planting came to life.

Next, he prayed for five Indian men in north India to apply what he had learned. God answered his prayer, but it was two years before they planted the first church using the new methodology. Meanwhile, David's mission agency was raising questions about the lack of results. His job was on the line.

Then, in one year they saw eight churches planted. The next year there were forty-eight new churches planted. By the fifth year, more than one thousand were planted. His mission couldn't believe it, so they conducted a formal survey of the work and found David's team had underestimated the number of new churches. By 2004 the work was entirely indigenously led, and David was no longer needed. In 2008 another survey showed that eighty thousand churches had been planted and two million people baptized. Since that time, Watson's training, coaching and writing has been a catalyst for disciple-making movements throughout the world.

APOSTOLIC POWER IN WEAKNESS

Paul was qualified and competent to be an apostle; his sufficiency came from God, who reveals his power through weakness. To imitate Paul is to receive the fullness of God's power in weakness. Weakness and power are at the heart of the gospel. They are the beginning and end of Paul's apostolic ministry. This is the life of every disciple. Paul proclaimed and lived the reality of the death and resurrection of Christ, and he wanted his disciples to experience that same reality.

True apostolic authority has nothing to do with office or status. It rejects personal gain as a motivation for ministry. Paul used his authority as a pioneer to bring others into the power of Jesus' death and resurrection. When disciples stand in that power, they share in the same authority the apostle possesses. When they stray from that power, the apostle brings correction to the body of Christ, and even to a fellow apostle. Apostolic authority is a gift to be given away.

Movement pioneers suffer with every other believer. However, apostolic ministry is uniquely characterized by suffering. Suffering marked the whole of Paul's missionary career. On the road to Damascus, his apostolic call was at the same time a call to suffering. The Lord spoke to Ananias about Paul, "This man is my chosen instrument to proclaim my name to the Gentiles and their kings and to the people of Israel. I will show him how much he must suffer for my name" (Acts 9:15-16). Even the last stage of Paul's mission was marked by a revelation from the Spirit that prison and hardship awaited him in every city (Acts 20:23).

Paul regarded suffering as the normal experience of a genuine apostle. While in the church God appointed apostles "first of all" (1 Corinthians 12:28), he has at the same time put them on display last of all like men condemned to die (1 Corinthians 4:9-13). The genuine apostle shares in the sufferings of Christ and the power of the resurrection.

The Corinthians were impressed with those who displayed signs of spiritual power, both through their eloquence and miracles. Paul could match these wonder workers with his own share of "signs, wonders and miracles" (2 Corinthians 12:11-12), but he regarded his apostolic sufferings as even more important in establishing his credentials. He devotes more space to describing his sufferings than any other sign of apostleship. According to Paul, apostleship brings with it a special call to take up one's cross and follow Christ.

This is because the only true foundation of the church is Jesus Christ. All other foundations will crumble or melt away in the face of the fire of God's judgment (1 Corinthians 3:11-13). Both the apostle and the churches are subject to the gospel.[3] Therefore, the apostle must remain true to the message of the cross, not only in terms of its content but also in the manner in which an apostle's life and ministry are conducted.

Paul summed up the nature of his ministry by saying, "I face death every day" (1 Corinthians 15:31). The apostle's legitimacy is not found in the power of his personality, in his spiritual experiences or in his commissioning by the right church authorities. Apostolic legitimacy is found only "in the extent to which his life and preaching represent the crucified Jesus."[4]

In the ministry of establishing new churches the apostle must not only proclaim truthfully the word of the cross but also live it. The foundation of any movement of disciples and churches must be Christ, not the wisdom and power of this world (1 Corinthians 1:22-23).

Paul discovered that the glory and power of God was revealed through his daily experience of death. Even when Paul experienced profound encounters with the power of God, he recalls,

"I was given a thorn in my flesh, a messenger of Satan, to torment me" (2 Corinthians 12:7-10). The Lord's response to Paul's repeated cries for deliverance was, "My grace is sufficient for you, for my power is made perfect in weakness" (v. 9). Paul learned to delight in his weaknesses, in insults, in hardships, in persecutions, in difficulties. The outcome was that Christ's power rested on him. "For when I am weak, then I am strong" (v. 10).

As a movement pioneer Paul learned to embrace his weakness and let God's power work through him. The living reality of union with Jesus Christ was at the heart of his faith. Salvation consists of being united with Christ in his death and resurrection. Through his weakness Paul led the way in discovering the power of God.

Paul's whole mission was seen in terms of miracle. He experienced the Spirit's leading, release from prison, deliverance from enemies and danger, signs and wonders, and raising the dead. All these events were an essential part of his apostolic witness and mission. They were the signs that the new age had begun.[5]

The miracles Paul and others performed in their apostolic ministries were common knowledge. He wrote, "I will not venture to speak of anything except what Christ has accomplished through me in leading the Gentiles to obey God by what I have said and done—by the power of signs and wonders, through the power of the Spirit" (Romans 15:18-19; cf. 1 Corinthians 2:4-5; Galatians 3:1-5; 1 Thessalonians 1:5-6; Acts 10:37-38; Hebrews 2:1-4).

For Paul the gospel was God's power revealed through the resurrection of Christ and evidenced through the presence of the Spirit.[6] He expected his ministry to be marked by the powerful presence and visible manifestations of the Spirit. The

churches that he founded were characterized by concrete and
visible manifestations of God's power through the Holy Spirit.
Paul could not have imagined conducting his ministry or living
the Christian life without dependence on the reality of the
power of God. New Testament believers experienced the Spirit
in powerful and visible ways.[7]

Paul reminded the Corinthians that their existence as a body
of believers was a miracle achieved by the Spirit of the living
God. And although Paul brought the gospel and started that
church, Paul's competence as a movement pioneer came from
God, not from himself (2 Corinthians 3:1-6).

For Paul "knowing Christ" meant to know both the power
of his resurrection and the fellowship of his sufferings (Philippians 3:10). His letters show how the Spirit was a source of
power in the midst of hardship.[8] Apostolic ministry embraced
these two realities—the weakness and shame of the cross and
the power and victory of the resurrection with the new age of
the Spirit.

An apostolic ministry with power but devoid of the cross has
no integrity. An apostolic ministry that embraces weakness
without the corresponding power of the Spirit will have integrity, but little impact.

Movement pioneers see cities, regions and nations. They
make bold, audacious plans. Along the way they will face
hardship and disappointment, opposition and delay. At times
they may feel abandoned by God and alone. They will also see
the power of God at work. Prayers will be answered. God's provision will come at the very last moment. Workers will be mo-
bilized. The gospel will spread. History will be made. There is a
price to pay, and it's worth it.

NOW WE CAN LEAVE BECAUSE OF ALL OF YOU

Peter and Saeng, a married couple, served as movement pioneers in a rural district in a small Asian nation under communist rule. Peter had access to the area as a development project leader. (To protect local believers, I can say no more.⁹)Through his fieldwork Peter met Daw, a respected figure in his village. On one occasion Peter felt prompted to visit Daw in his home.

Peter stepped into the dimly lit house and looked around. Most of the leading men of the village were there. Daw, deep in the gyrations of a sword dance, was performing one of the traditional spirit ceremonies of his people. After the ceremony, one of the village elders invited Peter into the house and said, "We have heard from the government to avoid Jesus, but we know that is something you believe, so tell us what is Jesus all about." That question led to hours of discussion, and as they talked the whole village heard the gospel. Daw listened, but gave no indication that he was deeply moved. In July 1997, however, Daw committed his life to following Christ.

The change in Daw's life was dramatic. He gave up drinking and stopped beating his wife. That got her attention. She too wanted to know Christ. It also drew the attention of everyone in his village.

At various locations outside of Daw's village, Peter met regularly with Daw to share stories about Jesus and taught chronologically from Genesis to Christ, helping Daw discover and follow Jesus for himself. Peter also modeled a gospel presentation, baptism and other basic lessons. Peter taught Daw to share his story and the gospel story with his family and friends. Early in 1999 eleven families believed and were baptized.

Peter refused to take responsibility to baptize and teach these new believers. Instead, he met with Daw and taught him Bible stories. Each story helped Daw take another step of obedience as a disciple of Jesus. Then Daw would return to his family and his village to teach the new believers. Along with seven elders the local believers appointed, Daw, not Peter, became the leader of the newly formed church.

It's a wonderful story of the power of the gospel. But it came with a price. Peter and Saeng had to leave behind the comforts of living in a Western nation to move to Southeast Asia. They had to learn language and culture. They had to raise a family in a place with no telephones, where electricity was available only two hours a day, where water was collected by dropping a bucket down a well, where there was no reasonable medical care and no road access during the rainy season.

During this time the health of Peter and Saeng's nine-month-old son took a serious downturn. A local doctor confirmed he had spinal meningitis. Their son needed urgent medical attention in the capital. The next flight was in three days. They gathered together with coworkers, laid hands on their son and prayed for healing, knowing that prayer was their only hope. He recovered.

Yet even these trying experiences were overshadowed by the price that the local believers paid for their newfound faith. The government was vehemently opposed to the Christian faith. In April 1999 the local governor forced recantations and then later arrested and imprisoned the seven elders of the church. They spent months in prison, but their faith grew.

Over fifteen years Peter and Saeng saw around forty believers with whom they regularly worked put in prison, where they had to survive on a minimal daily allowance of rice. The government targeted church leaders. A local movement pioneer was jailed four times. During one imprisonment he was beaten so severely that the right side of his skull was fractured and he sustained some brain damage.

The persecution didn't end with imprisonment and beatings. Eight believers were murdered. One believer was shot dead by an assassin in front of his young daughter. Another was beheaded. There were two cases of forced disappearance with no word of their whereabouts. Daw, his wife and child were taken on July 2, 2004, and never seen again.

Persecution took a terrible toll on the lives of these new believers. Some churches, like Daw's, barely survived. Others continued to spread the gospel and plant new churches in unreached villages, despite the imprisonment of their leaders. By 2007 there were around five thousand believers in one hundred new churches. Some of those churches were third generation.

After fifteen years of ministry it was time for Peter and Saeng to leave their adopted homeland. God had used them to spark a movement of disciples and churches in a harsh and violent land. God raised up movement pioneers from among the people to carry on the work.

Two hundred believers gathered to say goodbye. They represented the thousands across the land who could not attend but had found salvation through Christ. As they celebrated what God had done, one young man, a new believer, asked, "But why are you leaving now?" Peter replied, "We can leave because of all of you and the legacy that lives on in you."

Peter and Saeng relocated to a neighboring country, which enables them to continue to train and develop workers in the country they left and in other Asian nations. They paid a price to see the gospel spread in an unreached nation. God gave them the strength to endure. For all eternity they will celebrate the victories he won through them and the believers of their adopted homeland.

Movement pioneers, like the apostles, are "the first" and "the last." They are the first because they lead where the gospel has not yet gone. They see unreached peoples, cities and nations. They are last because their lives and ministries must conform to the message they bring. Their authority flows from the gospel, which is God's power revealed in the weakness of the cross. They of all people must learn the secret of God's power revealed in their weaknesses.

HOW THIS ENDS

We know how history ends. Jesus the obedient Son conquers all to the glory of God the Father. The Lamb that was slain has won persons from every tribe and language and people and nation. Worthy is the Lamb! This is the reality to which all things are headed. The Alpha and Omega will make all things new, and God will dwell with his people. These things are certain, more certain than the rising and setting of the sun.

By his grace the living Lord calls us into his mission. We live in the overlap of the ages. We struggle and stumble. We have this treasure in jars of clay to show that the all-surpassing power is from God, not from us. The gospel will go to the ends of the earth. The giants will fall. God will triumph, and wherever he does the fruit will be new disciples and new churches.

Until the end the coming King calls movement pioneers to lead the way. Will we follow?

Acknowledgments

I want to thank the many movement pioneers who have inspired me. Some of them are mentioned by name in this book. Others need to remain anonymous. They're my heroes. I love to tell their stories and share their lessons. I wish I could do what they do, but maybe then I wouldn't have time to tell their stories.

I want to acknowledge Nathan Shank and Jeff Sundell, two movement pioneers who have allowed me to get close to the action. They have freely shared their experience and time. Their input has made this a much better book.

Thank you to Angie Sundell and Val Gresham for proofreading and editorial input. You both kept me encouraged and kept me going.

To my most loyal and fearless critic—Grant Morrison. This is the third time you've been my companion on the journey of writing a book.

To Peter Bergmeier, my designer, who worked on the maps and a new version of the Movements Diamond.

Thanks to Helen Lee, my editor at IVP. She cared enough to challenge the early drafts of this book. The final result was worth the angst.

Michelle, thank you for everything.

Finally, this book is dedicated to someone who for decades has been a brother, a mentor and a trainer of movement pioneers all over the world. Because you'd like to remain anonymous, I'll just call you "Bill Smith."

Appendix

Discovery Bible Study and Three-Thirds Discipleship

Discovery Bible Study is a simple and immediately transferrable obedience-oriented method of making disciples. The method is profound because the Holy Spirit is present even when new disciples gather around the living Word of God to learn and obey.

Discovery Bible Study is effective in discipling people to conversion, in foundational discipleship and in long-term discipleship. It is a core component of church-planting movements throughout the world.

Here is one example of Discovery Bible Study within a Three-Thirds Discipleship framework. This outline can be adapted for meeting with seekers for foundational and long-term discipleship. It can also form the outline of how a new church gathers together. How have people been obeying what they learned last time? Has anyone shared the passage with someone?

FIRST THIRD: LOOK BACK

1. Care.

- Share any highlights or lowlights from the time since you last met.

- Pray for one another.

2. Worship God together in a simple and relevant way.

3. Ask questions for accountability.

- Following: How did you obey the lesson from last time?

- Fishing: Did you pray with anyone who was in need? Did you share a Bible story, your story or Jesus' story? Did you find a person of peace?

4. Cast vision.

- Take a few moments to cast vision for reaching lost people and making disciples.

- Pray for people you know who are far from God.

SECOND THIRD: LOOK UP

5. Read the new passage. Without looking at the text, retell the passage in your own words. Ask

- What does the passage teach us about God and/or Jesus?

- What does it teach us about people?

- Is there a command to obey or an example to follow?

FINAL THIRD: LOOK FORWARD

6. Practice a skill related to obeying what you have learned.

7. Set goals and pray. Ask

- What do you need to do this week to obey what you've learned?

- With whom could you share this passage, your story or the gospel story?

For more on Discovery Bible Study, see David L. Watson and Paul D. Watson, *Contagious Disciple Making: Leading Others on a Journey of Discovery* (Nashville: Thomas Nelson, 2014).

For more on Three-Thirds Discipleship, see Steve Smith with Ying Kai, *T4T: A Discipleship Re-Revolution* (Monument, CO: WIGTake Resources, 2011).

Notes

CHAPTER ONE: MOVEMENT PIONEERS LEAD FROM THE INSIDE OUT

[1]For more on Jeff Sundell see Steve Addison, *What Jesus Started: Joining the Movement, Changing the World* (Downers Grove, IL: InterVarsity Press, 2012), 55-59.

[2]See the appendix for more information on Discovery Bible Study.

[3]For more on "Following and Fishing" visit the movements.net website at www.movements.net/resources/following-fishing. There are many other functional equivalents to the Following and Fishing training. For training in the United States visit the No Place Left website at noplaceleft.net.

CHAPTER TWO: JESUS, OUR APOSTLE AND PIONEER

[1]Andreas J. Köstenberger, *The Missions of Jesus and the Disciples According to the Fourth Gospel: With Implications for the Fourth Gospel's Purpose and the Mission of the Contemporary Church* (Grand Rapids: Eerdmans, 1998), 107.

[2]Ibid., 194.

[3]A. F. Walls, "Apostle," in *The New Bible Dictionary*, ed. J. D. Douglas (Grand Rapids: Eerdmans, 1962), 48. For a more detailed examination of the biblical foundations for apostolic ministry see Stephen B. Addison, "The Continuing Ministry of the Apostle in the Church's Mission" (DMin diss., Fuller Theological Seminary, 1995), www.movements.net/2011/06/17/apostolic-ministry.html.

[4]When Judas forfeited his place among them, Matthias was chosen to replace him. However, when James died, no successor was chosen. In Acts 1:21-26 the qualifications for the successor were that he was with the band of disciples since the beginning of Jesus' ministry and that he was a witness of the resurrection.

[5]T. W. Manson, *The Church's Ministry* (London: Hodder & Stoughton, 1948), 54.

[6]J. B. Lightfoot, *The Epistle of St. Paul to the Galatians* (Grand Rapids: Zondervan, 1957), 95.

[7]See Howard A. Snyder, *The Community of the King* (Downers Grove, IL: InterVarsity Press, 1975), 87.

[8]It is possible that the Ephesians 4:11 reference to "pastors and teachers" refers to the one leadership gift of "pastor-teacher." For a discussion of the relationship between the leadership gifts in Ephesians 4, see Neil Cole, *Primal Fire: Reigniting the Church with the Five Gifts of Jesus* (Carol Stream, IL: Tyndale Momentum, 2014). See also Alan Hirsch and Tim Catchim, *The Permanent Revolution: Apostolic Imagination and Practice for the 21st Century Church* (San Francisco: Jossey-Bass, 2012).

[9]Gordon D. Fee, *The First Epistle to the Corinthians*, New International Commentary on the New Testament (Grand Rapids: Eerdmans, 1987), 619-20.

[10]Twice Paul used apostle to refer to a third group made up of church delegates, who were not primarily missionaries (2 Corinthians 8:23; Philippians 2:25). C. K. Barrett finds in the New Testament up to "eight persons, or groups of persons, all denoted, with varying degrees of propriety, by the term 'apostle' . . . and probably all giving it somewhat differing meaning" (C. K. Barrett, *The Signs of An Apostle* [London: Epworth Press, 1970], 71).

CHAPTER THREE: PETER, FIRST AMONG THE APOSTLES

[1]Markus Bockmuehl, *Simon Peter in Scripture and Memory: The New Testament Apostle in the Early Church* (Grand Rapids: Baker, 2012), Kindle edition, loc. 308.

[2]Ibid., loc. 262.

[3]Many have denied that Jesus referred to Peter as the rock on which he will build his church. Peter is a "stone," and Jesus or Peter's confession of Jesus is the "rock" Jesus will build on. D. A. Carson makes a convincing case for Peter as the "rock" and comments, "Yet if it were not for Protestant reactions against extremes of Roman Catholic interpretation, it is doubtful whether many would have taken 'rock' to be anything or anyone other than Peter" (D. A. Carson, "Matthew," in *Matthew, Mark, Luke*, Expositors' Bible Commentary 8, ed. Frank E. Gaebelein [Grand Rapids: Zondervan, 1984], 367-68).

[4]Pickled fish from Galilee were sold in Jerusalem. They were also sold to the Roman army of occupation and exported to other regions of the empire. See Michael Grant, *Saint Peter: A Biography* (New York: Scribner, 1995), 56.

[5]See Larry R. Helyer, *The Life and Witness of Peter* (Downers Grove, IL: IVP Academic, 2012), 24-27.

[6]See Acts 4:13 translated by Eckhard J. Schnabel, *Acts*, Zondervan Exegetical Commentary on the New Testament, ed. Clinton E. Arnold (Grand Rapids: Zondervan, 2012), 242.

[7]In Capernaum, there is archaeological evidence of a church building from the fourth century that is built on top of a first-century house where a church met. It is possible this was Peter's house. See Eckhard J. Schnabel, *Early Christian Mission: Jesus and the Twelve* (Downers Grove, IL: IVP Academic, 2004), 1:206. For Capernaum as Jesus' base, see Matthew 4:13; 8:5-13; Luke 7:1-10; John 4:46.

[8]See ibid., 188.

[9]There are clear parallels with the instructions he gave to the seventy-two before sending them out on mission (Luke 10) and Jesus' encounter with Zacchaeus (Luke 19). See David Lertis Matson, *Household Conversion Narratives in Acts: Pattern and Interpretation* (Sheffield, UK: Sheffield Academic Press, 1996), 224.

[10]The one exception is Paul's address to the Ephesian elders in Acts 20:13-38.

[11]We don't know who first brought the gospel to Rome. It is likely that Jewish pilgrims returning from Jerusalem started the churches planted there.

[12]See Schnabel, *Early Christian Mission*, 420.

[13]Ibid., 693.

[14]Oscar Cullmann, *Peter: Disciple, Apostle, Martyr*, 2nd ed. (Waco, TX: Baylor University Press, 2011), 41.

[15]Ibid., 913.

PIONEER PROFILE: HUDSON TAYLOR

[1]See Ralph D. Winter, "Four Men, Three Eras, Two Transitions: Modern Missions," in *Perspectives on the World Christian Movement: A Reader*, ed. Ralph D. Winter and Steven C. Hawthorne, 3rd ed. (Pasadena, CA: William Carey Library, 1999), 253-61.

[2]For this and subsequent quotes see James Hudson Taylor, *A Retrospect*, 3rd ed. (Toronto: China Inland Mission, 1902), 119-20, www.gutenberg.org/files/26744/26744-h/26744-h.htm.

[3]Ralph Winter, *The Unfolding Drama of the Christian Movement* (Pasadena, CA: Institute of International Studies, 1979), 20-21.

[4]See Stephen Neill, *A History of Christian Missions* (Harmondsworth, UK: Penguin Books, 1964), 333-34.

⁵James Hudson Taylor, quoted in Roger Steer, *J. Hudson Taylor: A Man in Christ* (Singapore: OMF, 1990), 211.

⁶For these and other figures on the growth of the China Inland Mission see Kenneth Scott Latourette, *The Great Century in Northern Africa and Asia A.D. 1800–A.D. 1914*, vol. 6 of A History of the Expansion of Christianity (London: Eyre & Spottiswoode, 1941), 326–31.

⁷Although Taylor didn't publish until 1886–1887, they became friends in Ningbo from 1855. See Christopher E. M. Wigram, "The Bible and Mission in Faith Perspective: J. Hudson Taylor and the Early China Inland Mission" (PhD diss., Utrecht University, 2007), 200, http://dspace.library.uu.nl/handle/1874/23085.

CHAPTER FOUR: STRUCTURING FOR MOVEMENTS

¹The spread of the Christian faith throughout the Roman Empire is well documented. For the spread of Christianity beyond the Roman Empire see Philip Jenkins, *The Lost History of Christianity: The Thousand-Year Golden Age of the Church in the Middle East, Africa and Asia—and How It Died* (New York: HarperOne, 2008).

²See Richard Fletcher, *The Conversion of Europe: From Paganism to Christianity 371–1386 A.D.* (London: Fontana Press, 1998), 26–27.

³Mark A. Noll, *Turning Points: Decisive Moments in the History of Christianity* (Grand Rapids: Baker Academic, 2012), 78.

⁴Paul D. L. Avis, *The Church in the Theology of the Reformers*, New Foundations Theological Library, ed. Peter Toon and Ralph P. Martin (Atlanta: John Knox Press, 1981), 170.

⁵Charles Wesley Ranson, *That the World May Know* (Whitefish, MT: Literary Licensing, 2012), 65.

⁶Arthur F. Glasser, "The Apostle Paul and the Missionary Task," in *Perspectives on the World Christian Movement: A Reader*, ed. Ralph D. Winter and Steven C. Hawthorne, 3rd ed. (Pasadena, CA: William Carey Library, 1999), 130.

⁷Paul Pierson, *The Dynamics of Christian Mission: History Through a Missiological Perspective* (Pasadena, CA: William Carey Library, 2009), 40, http://library.wciu.edu/ebooks/Paul_Pierson_E/Dynamics_of_Christian_Mission_Whole_book.pdf.

⁸Paul knows he has an apostolic right to be supported by the churches (1 Corinthians 9:3-12), but refuses financial support when it compromises the spread of the gospel. "Paul refuses to invoke an authority which is right-

fully his in order to submit himself to a greater authority, the demand of the gospel" (John Howard Schutz, *Paul and the Anatomy of Apostolic Authority* [Louisville, KY: Westminster John Knox, 2007], 235).

[9]Ralph D. Winter, "The Two Structures of God's Redemptive Mission," in Winter and Hawthorne, *Perspectives on the World Christian Movement*, 220-30. For more on the two structures, both for and against, see Joseph C. and Michele C., "Field Governed Mission Structures, Part 1: In the New Testament," *International Journal of Frontier Missions* 18, no. 2 (2001): 59-66; Harold R. Cook, "Who Really Sent the First Missionaries?" *Evangelical Missions Quarterly* 13 (1975): 233-40; Arthur F. Glasser, "The Apostle Paul and the Missionary Task," in Winter and Hawthorne, *Perspectives on the World Christian Movement*, 127-34; Samuel F. Metcalf, "When Local Churches Act Like Agencies: A Fresh Look at Mission Agency-Local Church Relationships," *Evangelical Missions Quarterly* 29, no. 2 (1993): 142-49; Edward F. Murphy, "The Missionary Society as an Apostolic Team," *Missiology* 4, no. 1 (1976): 103-18; Mark Vanderwerf, "The Two Structures of God's Mission," *Global Missiology* 3, no. 8 (2011), ojs.globalmissiology.org/index.php/english/article/view/589/1493.

[10]See Pierson, *Dynamics of Christian Mission*, 40.

[11]For a critique of Ralph Winter, see Bruce Camp, "A Theological Examination of the Two-Structure Theory," *Missiology* 23, no. 2 (1995): 197-209.

[12]Howard Snyder writes, "Since the church is itself a missionary community, any group of missionaries may be a legitimate embodiment of the church. There can be no question of the church versus missionary structures. Wherever Christians are, there is the church, and there believers are responsible for demonstrating the reality of Christian community. . . . Missionaries can never go to another culture and leave the Church behind!" (Howard A. Snyder, *The Community of the King* [Downers Grove, IL: InterVarsity Press, 1975], 193).

[13]See Steve Addison, *Movements That Change the World*, 87-92.

[14]John Howard Schutz, *Paul and the Anatomy of Apostolic Authority* (Louisville, KY: Westminster John Knox, 2007), 250.

CHAPTER FIVE: NO PLACE LEFT IN SOUTH ASIA

[1]Information for this chapter was collected through interviews conducted by the author with Nathan Shank, Lipok and Kumar on February 3-5, 2014.

[2]Nathan Shank and Kari Shank, "Four Fields of Kingdom Growth: Starting

and Releasing Healthy Churches," *Movements.net*, rev. 2014, www.move ments.net/4fields2014.

[3]I tell Lipok's story in Steve Addison, *What Jesus Started* (Downers Grove, IL: InterVarsity Press, 2012), 185-86. See also "Entire Communities Being Transformed," *East-West* (blog), December 13, 2010, www.eastwest.org/blog/ entire-communities-being-transformed-2.

[4]This is a conservative estimate; the precise number of churches is hard to verify.

PIONEER PROFILE: WILLIAM TAYLOR

[1]For the details on Taylor's life and ministry see David Bundy, "Bishop William Taylor and Methodist Mission: A Study in Nineteenth Century Social History," *Methodist History* 27, no. 4 (1989): 197-210; and David Bundy, "Bishop William Taylor and Methodist Mission: A Study in Nineteenth Century Social History, Part 2, Social Structures in Collision," *Methodist History* 28, no. 1 (1989): 3-21.

[2]David Hempton, *Methodism: Empire of the Spirit* (New Haven, CT: Yale University Press, 2005), 171-72.

[3]See Walter J. Hollenweger, "Methodism's Past in Pentecostalism's Present: A Case Study of a Cultural Clash in Chile," *Methodist History* 20 (1982): 169-82, http://archives.gcah.org/xmlui/bitstream/handle/10516/587/Meth odist-History-07-1982-Hollenweger.pdf?sequence=1.

[4]Ibid., 170.

[5]Bundy, "Social Structures in Collision," 12-13.

CHAPTER SIX: FIVE LEVELS OF MOVEMENT LEADERSHIP

[1]Nathan Shank and Kari Shank, "Four Fields of Kingdom Growth: Starting and Releasing Healthy Churches," *Movements.net*, rev. 2014, 108-15, www .movements.net/4fields2014. See also "Nathan Shank Unpacks the Five Levels of Movement Leadership," http://www.movements.net/shank-five-levels-of-movement-leadership.

[2]Steve Smith, "The Bare Essentials of Helping Groups Become Churches," *Mission Frontiers*, September 1, 2012, www.missionfrontiers.org/issue/ar ticle/the-bare-essentials-of-helping-groups-become-churches.

[3]On the question of whether new believers are qualified to lead in new churches, see Steve Smith, "The Bible on Church Planting Movements: Qualified to Lead?" *Mission Frontiers*, February 28, 2011, www.mission

frontiers.org/issue/article/the-bible-on-church-planting-movements.

[4]On the church in Crete, see Eckhard J. Schnabel, *Early Christian Mission: Jesus and the Twelve* (Downers Grove, IL: IVP Academic, 2004), 1:1283-87.

[5]See Nathan Shank, "Generational Mapping: Tracking Elements of Church Formation Within CPM's," *Mission Frontiers*, November-December 2012, 26-30, www.missionfrontiers.org/pdfs/34-6-generational-mapping.pdf; and Shank and Shank, "Four Fields of Kingdom Growth," 93-95.

[6]There are exceptions to this general principle. Some effective multiplication trainers "parachute in" without first gaining field experience as church multipliers.

[7]The Shanks identify six streams of new churches in Cyprus, Phrygia, Galatia, Macedonia, Achaia and Asia Minor (Shank and Shank, "Four Fields of Kingdom Growth," 124-30).

[8]Typically that investment is for the cost of travel and training, not salaries. Foreign funding is restricted because it normally results in dependency and control.

PIONEER PROFILE: VICTOR LANDERO

[1]Sources for Victor Landero's story are Edward F. Murphy, *Spiritual Gifts and the Great Commission* (Pasadena, CA: Mandate Press, 1975), 222-35; Leslie J. Thompson, "Establishment and Growth of Protestantism in Colombia" (PhD diss., University of Wales, 2005), 235-38, www.prolades.com/cra/regions/sam/col/thompson_thesis.pdf; David M. Howard and Bob Owen, *The Victor: The Victor Landero Story* (Old Tappan, NJ: Revell, 1979).

[2]See Philip Jenkins, *The Next Christendom: The Coming of Global Christianity* (New York: Oxford University Press, 2002), 53; and Steve Addison, *Movements That Change the World* (Downers Grove, IL: InterVarsity Press), 51-53.

CHAPTER SEVEN: NO PLACE LEFT IN AMERICA

[1]For an account of this lunch see Steve Addison, "Scattering to Gather," *Movements.net*, October 23, 2012, www.movements.net/2012/10/23/scattering-to-gather-part-one.html.

[2]I cover the early days of Jeff's ministry in Nepal and the United States in Steve Addison, *What Jesus Started* (Downers Grove, IL: InterVarsity Press, 2012), 55-59. See also Jeff Sundell, "4x4 Movements," *Mission Frontiers* 36, no. 2 (2014): 7-9, www.missionfrontiers.org/issue/article/4x4-movements-article.

[3]For examples of Jeff Sundell's training materials and methods visit 4fields.net.

[4]See Gary L. Stump, "From Gathering a Crowd to Making Disciples" and "I'm Seeing People Come to Christ in Numbers Unlike Anything I've Ever Seen in My Ministry," www.movements.net/resources/the-movements-podcast; see also Gary L. Stump, "No Longer 'Church as Usual,'" *Mission Frontiers* 36, no. 2 (2014): 15-16, www.missionfrontiers.org/issue/article/no-longer-church-as-usual.

[5]"Our Vision," *Onward Church,* accessed March 18, 2014, www.onward church.org/vision.

[6]See Steve Smith with Ying Kai, *T4T: A Discipleship Re-Revolution* (Monument, CO: WIGTake Resources, 2011). See also Addison, *What Jesus Started,* 106-9.

[7]Gary's training materials are available for others to use at "Documents," *Onward Church,* accessed March 18, 2014, www.onwardchurch.org/resources/documents/#.

[8]For an account of Paul's ministry in Ephesus and the impact on Asia Minor, see Addison, *What Jesus Started,* 154-58.

[9]See the podcast interview with the Campbells at Steve Addison, "God, Give Us Austin Texas or We Die!" *Movements.net,* October 30, 2013, www.move ments.net/2013/10/30/god-give-us-austin-texas-or-we-die.html. See also, Fred Campbell and Melissa Campbell, "No Longer 'Business as Usual,'" *Mission Frontiers* 36, no. 2 (2014): 12-14, www.missionfrontiers.org/issue/article/no-longer-business-as-usual.

[10]For an outline of the strategy, visit movements.net/burrito-outreach.

[11]"Seven Commands of Christ" was developed by George Patterson as a foundational discipleship tool. See George Patterson and Richard Scoggins Patterson, *Church Multiplication Guide,* rev. ed. (Pasadena, CA: William Carey Library, 2003).

[12]Jesus told his disciples to seek out "houses of peace" when they enter a town (Luke 10:5-7). Houses of peace welcome the messenger and provide relational links for the gospel to spread to the rest of the community. For more on houses of peace, see Addison, *What Jesus Started,* 32-35.

[13]See the interview with Chuck Wood, "Chuck Wood's Cheesy Vision for San Antonio," *Movements.net,* www.movements.net/resources/the-move ments-podcast; see also Chuck Wood, "No Longer 'Discipleship as Usual,'" *Mission Frontiers* 36, no. 2 (2014): 17-18, www.missionfrontiers.org/issue/article/no-longer-discipleship-as-usual.

[14]See the 50-5-50 Network homepage at www.50-5-50network.com.

CHAPTER EIGHT: FROM CHURCH TO MOVEMENT

[1]See Steve Addison, "From (Immigrant) Church to Movement #1," *Movements.net*, September 8, 2014, www.movements.net/2014/09/08/from-immigrant-church-to-movement-1-podcast.html.

[2]See Steve Addison, "How Churches Can Spark Disciple Making Movements," *Movements.net*, August 7, 2014, www.movements.net/2014/08/07/how-churches-can-spark-disciple-making-movements-podcast.html; and Steve Addison, "From Church to Movement: Peter Snyman," *Movements.net*, September 29, 2014, www.movements.net/2014/09/29/from-church-to-movement-peter-snyman-podcast.html.

[3]See Steve Addison, "Church to Movement: Don Waybright," *Movements.net*, September 22, 2014, www.movements.net/2014/09/22/church-to-movement-don-waybright-podcast.html.

[4]See the Keystone Project homepage at www.keystoneproject.org.

[5]For more on Praxeis, see Steve Addison, "Interview with Dave Lawton of Praxeis," *Movements.net*, July 17, 2014, www.movements.net/2014/07/17/interview-with-dave-lawton-of-praxeis-podcast.html.

CHAPTER NINE: NO PLACE LEFT IN THE HOUSE OF ISLAM

[1]This information about Hussain comes from a March 2, 2015, interview with Bill Smith. For security reasons, names and exact location are not identified in any of the examples cited in this chapter.

[2]Muslims make up 23 percent of the world's population, but their rate of population growth is about twice that of the world's non-Muslim population. See "The Future of the Global Muslim Population," Pew Research Center, accessed March 6, 2015, www.pewforum.org/2011/01/27/the-future-of-the-global-muslim-population.

[3]See David Garrison, *A Wind in the House of Islam: How God Is Drawing Muslims Around the World to Faith in Jesus Christ* (Monument, CO: WIGTake Resources, 2014), 18. Garrison defines a movement as one thousand baptisms or one hundred new church starts within twenty years (ibid., 5).

[4]See ibid., 117-21.

[5]Jerry Trousdale, interviewed by the author on March 5, 2015. See also Jerry Trousdale, *Miraculous Movements: How Hundreds of Thousands of Muslims Are Falling in Love with Jesus* (Nashville: Thomas Nelson, 2012), 125-26.

[6]For the full story see Trousdale, *Miraculous Movements*, 25-31.

[7]These three points are found in sura 3:42-55 of the Qur'an. For more on this

method of connecting with Muslims see Kevin Greeson, *The Camel: How Muslims Are Coming to Faith in Christ!* (Midlothian, VA: WIGTake Resources, 2007). Also Kevin Greeson, "Building a Gospel Bridge to Muslims," *Movements.net*, October 20, 2011, www.movements.net/?s=Building+A+Go spel+Bridge+to+Muslims.

[8]See sura 10:94.

[9]For more on this approach see, Trousdale, *Miraculous Movements*; and David L. Watson and Paul D. Watson, *Contagious Disciple Making: Leading Others on a Journey of Discovery* (Nashville: Thomas Nelson, 2014).

[10]Mike Shipman, interview with the author on March 19, 2015. See Mike Shipman, *Plan A: Simply Disciple the Whole World* (Richmond, VA: International Mission Board, 2015).

CHAPTER TEN: WHAT WOULD IT TAKE TO STOP YOU?

[1]David L. Watson and Paul D. Watson, *Contagious Disciple Making: Leading Others on a Journey of Discovery* (Nashville: Thomas Nelson, 2014).

[2]See Watson and Watson, *Contagious Disciple Making*, xi–xiv.

[3]John Howard Schutz, *Paul and the Anatomy of Apostolic Authority* (Louisville, KY: Westminster John Knox, 2007), 123.

[4]C. K. Barrett, *A Commentary on the Second Epistle to the Corinthians*, Black's New Testament Commentaries, ed. Henry Chadwick (London: Adam & Charles Black, 1973), 30. Schutz agrees, "Nothing is more closely associated with the 'apostle' than the 'gospel.' Paul cannot separate his calling as apostle from its purpose—to serve the gospel" (Schutz, *Paul and the Anatomy of Apostolic Authority*, 35).

[5]G. W. H. Lampe, "Miracles in the Acts of the Apostles," in *Miracles*, ed. C. F. D. Moule (London: A. R. Mowbray, 1965), 171.

[6]Gordon D. Fee, *God's Empowering Presence: The Holy Spirit in the Letters of Paul* (Peabody, MA: Hendrickson, 1994), 824.

[7]Ibid, 895.

[8]For the relationship between affliction and the Holy Spirit in Paul's writings, see Romans 15:18-19; 1 Corinthians 2:4-5; 2 Corinthians 4:7; 12:1-12; 13:3-4; Philippians 3:9-10; Colossians 1:29; 1 Thessalonians 1:5-6; 2 Timothy 1:6-8.

[9]Peter and Saeng, a missionary couple, have asked that their names not be revealed for security reasons.

Bibliography

Addison, Steve. "The Continuing Ministry of the Apostle in the Church's Mission." DMin diss., Fuller Theological Seminary, 1995. www.move ments.net/wp-content/uploads/2011/06/ApostolicMinistry-SteveAddison.pdf.

——. *Movements That Change the World: Five Keys to Spreading the Gospel*. Downers Grove, IL: InterVarsity Press, 2011.

——. *What Jesus Started: Joining the Movement, Changing the World*. Downers Grove, IL: InterVarsity Press, 2012.

Allen, Roland. *Missionary Methods: St. Paul's or Ours?* London: World Dominion Press, 1956.

Avis, Paul D. L. *The Church in the Theology of the Reformers*. New Foundations Theological Library. Atlanta: John Knox Press, 1981.

Barrett, C. K. *A Commentary on the Second Epistle to the Corinthians*. Black's New Testament Commentaries. London: Adam & Charles Black, 1973.

——. *The Signs of an Apostle*. London: Epworth Press, 1970.

Bockmuehl, Markus. *Simon Peter in Scripture and Memory: The New Testament Apostle in the Early Church*. Grand Rapids: Baker, 2012.

Bundy, David. "Bishop William Taylor and Methodist Mission: A Study in Nineteenth Century Social History." *Methodist History* 27, no. 4 (1989): 197-210.

——. "Bishop William Taylor and Methodist Mission: A Study in Nineteenth Century Social History, Part 2, Social Structures in Collision." *Methodist History* 28, no. 1 (1989): 3-21.

C., Joseph, and Michele C. "Field Governed Mission Structures, Part 1: In the New Testament." *International Journal of Frontier Missions* 18, no. 2 (2001): 59-66.

Camp, Bruce. "A Theological Examination of the Two-Structure Theory." *Missiology* 23, no. 2 (1995): 197-209.

Campbell, Fred, and Melissa Campbell. "No Longer 'Business as Usual.'" *Mission Frontiers* 36, no. 2 (2014): 12-14.

Carson, D. A. "Matthew." In *Matthew, Mark, Luke*. Expositors' Bible Commentary 8. Edited by Frank E. Gaebelein. Grand Rapids: Zondervan, 1984.

Cole, Neil. *Primal Fire: Reigniting the Church With the Five Gifts of Jesus*. Carol Stream, IL: Tyndale Momentum, 2014.

Cook, Harold R. "Who Really Sent the First Missionaries?" *Evangelical Missions Quarterly* 13 (1975): 233-40.

Cullmann, Oscar. *Peter: Disciple, Apostle, Martyr*. Translated by Floyd V. Filson. London: SCM, 1953.

Fee, Gordon D. *The First Epistle to the Corinthians*. New International Commentary on the New Testament. Grand Rapids: Eerdmans, 1987.

————. *God's Empowering Presence: The Holy Spirit in the Letters of Paul*. Peabody, MA: Hendrickson, 2009.

Fletcher, Richard. *The Conversion of Europe: From Paganism to Christianity 371-1386 A.D.* London: Fontana Press, 1998.

Garrison, David. *A Wind in the House of Islam: How God Is Drawing Muslims Around the World to Faith in Jesus Christ*. Monument CO: WIGTake Resources, 2014.

Glasser, Arthur F. "The Apostle Paul and the Missionary Task." In *Perspectives on the World Christian Movement: A Reader*. 3rd ed. Edited by Ralph D. Winter and Steven C. Hawthorne. Pasadena, CA: William Carey Library, 1999.

Grant, Michael. *Saint Peter: A Biography*. New York: Scribner, 1995.

Greeson, Kevin. *The Camel: How Muslims Are Coming to Faith in Christ!* Monument, CO: WIGTake Resources, 2010.

Helyer, Larry R. *The Life and Witness of Peter*. Downers Grove, IL: IVP Academic, 2012.

Hempton, David. *Methodism: Empire of the Spirit*. New Haven, CT: Yale University Press, 2005.

Hengel, Martin. *Saint Peter: The Underestimated Apostle*. Translated by

Thomas H. Trapp. Grand Rapids: Eerdmans, 2010.

Hirsch, Alan, and Dave Ferguson. *On the Verge: A Journey Into the Apostolic Future of the Church*. Grand Rapids: Zondervan, 2011.

Hirsch, Alan, and Tim Catchim. *The Permanent Revolution: Apostolic Imagination and Practice for the 21st Century Church*. San Francisco: Jossey-Bass, 2012.

Hollenweger, Walter J. "Methodism's Past in Pentecostalism's Present: A Case Study of a Cultural Clash in Chile." *Methodist History* 20 (1982): 169-82.

Howard, David M., and Bob Owen. *The Victor: The Victor Landero Story*. Old Tappan, NJ: Revell, 1979.

Jenkins, Philip. *The Lost History of Christianity: The Thousand-Year Golden Age of the Church in the Middle East, Africa and Asia—and How It Died*. New York: HarperOne, 2008.

———. *The Next Christendom: The Coming of Global Christianity*. New York: Oxford University Press, 2002.

Köstenberger, Andreas J. *The Missions of Jesus and the Disciples According to the Fourth Gospel: With Implications for the Fourth Gospel's Purpose and the Mission of the Contemporary Church*. Grand Rapids: Eerdmans, 1998.

Lampe, G. W. H. "Miracles in the Acts of the Apostles." In *Miracles*. Edited by C. F. D. Moule. London: A. R. Mowbray, 1965.

Latourette, Kenneth Scott. *The Great Century in Northern Africa and Asia A.D. 1800-A.D. 1914*. A History of the Expansion of Christianity 6. London: Eyre & Spottiswoode, 1941.

Lightfoot, J. B. *The Epistle of St. Paul to the Galatians*. Grand Rapids: Zondervan, 1957.

Manson, T. W. *The Church's Ministry*. London: Hodder & Stoughton, 1948.

Matson, David Lertis. *Household Conversion Narratives in Acts: Pattern and Interpretation*. Sheffield, UK: Sheffield Academic Press, 1996.

Metcalf, Samuel F. "When Local Churches Act Like Agencies: A Fresh Look At Mission Agency-Local Church Relationships." *Evangelical Missions Quarterly* 29, no. 2 (1993): 142-49.

Metcalf, Sam. *Beyond the Local Church: How Apostolic Movements Can Change the World*. Downers Grove, IL: InterVarsity Press, 2015.

Murphy, Edward F. *Spiritual Gifts and the Great Commission*. Pasadena, CA: Mandate Press, 1975.

———. "The Missionary Society as an Apostolic Team." *Missiology* 4, no. 1 (1976): 103-18.

Neill, Stephen. *A History of Christian Missions*. Harmondsworth, UK: Penguin Books, 1964.

Newbigin, Lesslie. *The Household of God: Lectures on the Nature of Church*. London: SCM, 1957.

Noll, Mark A. *Turning Points: Decisive Moments in the History of Christianity*. Leicester: Inter-Varsity Press, 1997.

Patterson, George, and Richard Scoggins. *Church Multiplication Guide*. Pasadena, CA: William Carey Library, 2003.

Pierson, Paul. *The Dynamics of Christian Mission: History Through a Missiological Perspective*. Pasadena, CA: William Carey Library, 2009.

Ranson, C. W. *That the World May Know*. New York: Friendship Press, 1953.

Schnabel, Eckhard J. *Acts*. Zondervan Exegetical Commentary on the New Testament. Grand Rapids: Zondervan, 2012.

———. *Early Christian Mission: Jesus and the Twelve*. Downers Grove, IL: IVP Academic, 2004.

———. *Early Christian Mission: Paul and the Early Church*. Downers Grove, IL: IVP Academic, 2004.

———. "Mission, Early Non-Pauline." In *Dictionary of the Later New Testament and Its Developments*. Edited by Ralph P. Martin and Peter H. Davids. Downers Grove, IL: IVP Academic, 1997.

———. *Paul the Missionary: Realities, Strategies and Methods*. Downers Grove, IL: IVP Academic, 2008.

Schutz, John Howard. *Paul and the Anatomy of Apostolic Authority*. Louisville, KY: Westminster John Knox, 2007.

Shank, Nathan, and Kari Shank. "Four Fields of Kingdom Growth: Starting and Releasing Healthy Churches." Movements.net, 2007; rev. 2014. www.movements.net/4fields2014.

Shank, Nathan. "Generational Mapping: Tracking Elements of Church Formation Within CPMs." *Mission Frontiers*, November-December 2012, 26-30. www.missionfrontiers.org/pdfs/34-6-generational-mapping.pdf.

Shipman, Mike. *Any 3: Anyone, Anywhere, Any Time: Lead Muslims to Christ Now!* Monument CO: WIGTake Resources, 2013.

———. *Plan A: Simply Disciple the Whole World.* Richmond, VA: International Mission Board, 2015.

Smith, Steve. "The Bare Essentials of Helping Groups Become Churches." *Mission Frontiers*, September–October 2012, 22–25.

———. "Qualified to Lead?" *Mission Frontiers*, February 28, 2011. www.missionfrontiers.org/issue/article/the-bible-on-church-planting-movements.

Smith, Steve, with Ying Kai. *T4T: A Discipleship Re-Revolution.* Monument, CO: WIGTake Resources, 2011.

Stump, Gary. "No Longer 'Church as Usual.'" *Mission Frontiers* 36, no. 2 (2014): 15–16. www.missionfrontiers.org/issue/article/no-longer-church-as-usual.

Snyder, Howard A. *The Community of the King.* Downers Grove, IL: InterVarsity Press, 1975.

Steer, Roger. *J. Hudson Taylor: A Man in Christ.* Wheaton, IL: Harold Shaw, 1993.

Sundell, Jeff. "4x4 Movements." *Mission Frontiers* 36, no. 2 (2014): 7–9. www.missionfrontiers.org/issue/article/4x4-movements-article.

Taylor, James Hudson. *A Retrospect.* Toronto: China Inland Mission, 1902. www.gutenberg.org/files/26744/26744-h/26744-h.htm.

Thompson, Leslie J. "Establishment and Growth of Protestantism in Colombia." PhD diss., University of Wales, 2005. www.prolades.com/cra/regions/sam/col/thompson_thesis.pdf.

Trousdale, Jerry. *Miraculous Movements: How Hundreds of Thousands of Muslims Are Falling in Love with Jesus.* Nashville: Thomas Nelson, 2012.

Vanderwerf, Mark. "The Two Structures of God's Mission." *Global Missiology* 3, no. 8 (2011).

Walls, A. F. "Apostle." In *The New Bible Dictionary.* Edited by J. D. Douglas. Downers Grove, IL: InterVarsity Press, 1962.

Watson, David. "Discovering God: Field Testing Guide, v2.0." *Movements .net.* 2008. www.movements.net/wp-content/uploads/2012/02/2008-Discovering-God-2.0.pdf.

Watson, David L., and Paul D. Watson. *Contagious Disciple Making: Leading Others on a Journey of Discovery*. Nashville: Thomas Nelson, 2014.

Wigram, Christopher E. M. "The Bible and Mission in Faith Perspective: J. Hudson Taylor and the Early China Inland Mission." PhD diss., Utrecht University, 2007.

Winter, Ralph D. "Four Men, Three Eras, Two Transitions: Modern Missions." In *Perspectives on the World Christian Movement: A Reader*. Edited by Ralph D. Winter and Steven C. Hawthorne. 3rd ed. Pasadena, CA: William Carey Library, 1999.

——. "The Two Structures of God's Redemptive Mission." In *Perspectives on the World Christian Movement: A Reader*. Edited by Ralph D. Winter and Steven C. Hawthorne. 3rd ed. Pasadena, CA: William Carey Library, 1999.

——. *The Unfolding Drama of the Christian Movement*. Pasadena, CA: Institute of International Studies, 1979.

Witherington, Ben. *The Acts of the Apostles: A Socio-Rhetorical Commentary*. Grand Rapids: Eerdmans, 1997.

Wood, Chuck. "No Longer 'Discipleship as Usual." *Mission Frontiers* 36, no. 2 (2014): 17-18. www.missionfrontiers.org/issue/archive/4x4-movements.

Other Books by Steve Addison

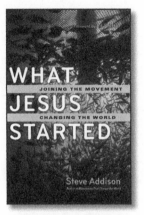

*Movements That
Change the World*
978-0-8308-3619-2

What Jesus Started
978-0-8308-6643-4

Stay in touch—find

- latest insights from Steve
- podcast interviews
- training events
- resources

and more at **movements.net**